T0295922

Generation Why

Generation Why

How Boomers Can Lead and Learn from Millennials and Gen Z

KARL MOORE

McGill-Queen's University Press

Montreal & Kingston • London • Chicago

© McGill-Queen's University Press 2023

ISBN 978-0-2280-1686-1 (cloth)
ISBN 978-0-2280-1687-8 (paper)
ISBN 978-0-2280-1813-1 (ePDF)
ISBN 978-0-2280-1814-8 (ePUB)

Legal deposit second quarter 2023
Bibliothèque nationale du Québec

Printed in Canada on acid-free paper that is 100% ancient forest
free (100% post-consumer recycled), processed chlorine free

We acknowledge the support of the Canada Council for the Arts.
Nous remercions le Conseil des arts du Canada de son soutien.

Library and Archives Canada Cataloguing in Publication

Title: Generation why : how boomers can lead and learn from
   millennials and gen Z / Karl Moore.
Names: Moore, Karl, 1955- author.
Description: Includes bibliographical references and index.
Identifiers: Canadiana (print) 20220491585 | Canadiana (ebook)
   20220491607 | ISBN 9780228016861 (cloth) | ISBN 9780228016878
   (paper) | ISBN 9780228018131 (ePDF) | ISBN 9780228018148
   (ePUB)
Subjects: LCSH: Personnel management. | LCSH: Work environ-
   ment. | LCSH: Generation Y—Employment. | LCSH: Generation
   Z—Employment. | LCSH: Young adults—Employment. | LCSH:
   Postmodernism.
Classification: LCC HF5549 .M635 2023 | DDC 658.4/092—dc23

Contents

Figures

Generation Why

Introduction

Renée rubbed her forehead. What a headache! Her team of twenty-some-thing-year-old analysts were intelligent and clearly talented, but awfully dif-ficult to work with at times. They didn't seem to understand the central fact of the situation: she was their boss and what she said, stood. Why was that so hard for them to understand? Their desires, after all, were completely unre-alistic. They wanted to work from home in a foreign country for months on end, check out every day at 5 p.m., or 6 p.m. at the latest, no matter the im-portance of the client or the amount of work remaining to be done. They ex-pected to be consulted on every decision she made and appeared to consider her twenty-year career as a hard-working lead investment banker as insignifi-cant. Did they realize just how difficult it had been for her to attend university (she had been the first in her family to do so, and against the wishes of her father), or to then search for and finally find a company bold enough to hire a woman in this highly competitive field? She had had nothing handed to her, but instead worked hard for every accomplishment. Now it was as if she had to justify her decision-making to her reports! It was as if her experience and wisdom were derived from some ancient period in history, thereby rendering them irrelevant. To add insult to injury, they persisted in making unreasonable demands and consistently tried to convince her that they were victims. In gen-eral, they treated her with less respect than she felt was her due, based on her experience, her track record, and her qualities as a manager.

Does Renée's situation sound all too familiar? Can you relate to her frustration? We believe that Renée has come face to face with the Millennial and Z generations (those under the age of thirty-five – give or take a few years); other names for this cohort include Generation Y, Echo Boomers, Net

Generation, etc. This book is not directly about their generation per se but rather about their worldview, and how it impacts their behaviour in a business or other organizational setting. Many excellent books, articles, and · newspapers have already been written about this generation, and some of my favourites are listed in the annotated bibliography. What sets this book apart is my focus on the Postmodern worldview and its impact on best practices for managing this cohort.

The majority of the material written about this generation is based on survey data and individual personal experiences related to the author. My approach with this book is different – I focus on this generation's worldview: the Postmodern worldview. My book highlights the critical fact that what university students are taught during pivotal years of their schooling very much influences their behaviour at work and their view of how they want to be led. Though, given their worldview, *led* may be too strong a word – even *manage* may be too strong. Perhaps it would be better to say, *worked with*.

To better understand the Millennial and Z generations, I believe it is helpful to look at their education and the underlying ideas that the education system taught them – that is, their Postmodern worldview. Rather than cover the whole of Postmodern thought, this book focuses on the aspects of their worldview that impact their perception of leadership and work. During the last years of high school, time at college, and then initial years in the workforce, our worldview is formed. Although it continues to evolve over time, these late-teen-early-twenties years provide a base for how we think. Events also matter. The tragedy of 9/11, the financial crisis of 2008, and the COVID-19 years: all affected people's thinking about life and leadership – though 9/11 not so much the former for Generation Zers, who are too young to have had clear memories of that day in 2001. My parents grew up during the Great Depression. It left an indelible mark on both of them. To her dying day, my mother would turn off every light as she left a room, not to save money at that point in her life, but because of having grown up during the 1930s. We aren't yet in the kind of economic recession that my parents, and those of countless others, experienced almost a century ago; however, members of Generation Z, those aged roughly twenty-six (in 2023) and younger, will have their worldview shaped by the COVID crisis that began in 2020 in much the same way. The literature suggests that the end of high school, university, and our early work years tend to have shaped our worldview significantly.[1] It evolves after that, but those years act as a solid foundation for how we respond in the remainder of our lives.

I graduated with an MBA from the University of Southern California (USC) in the late 1970s, a period of prosperity in Southern California. Everybody in our graduating class had multiple job offers. I had worked in my native Toronto for IBM for the summer and got offers from two different divisions. The good times rolled on for quite a while after I left university. There was a recession in the early 1980s, but I was in basic training for nine months at IBM at the time and we barely noticed it. By the time the next one rolled around in the early '90s, many boomers occupied reasonably safe positions. Life was kind to my generation, and we believed that we were supremely talented and that capitalism worked for us – all in all, we had a fairly sunny view of the world. Not everyone benefitted from such luck, but in much of the Western world it was good times early on in the careers of boomers.

That said, more fundamentally, a generation's worldview comes from what they are taught about such things as the nature of truth, the hierarchy of the world, and what it takes to be a leader. Beyond what we are taught, there is what we experience. Like my parents, perhaps the Depression or the Second World War impacted your elders to a considerable degree and for much of their working lives.

For Generation Z, the current global pandemic is likely a formative moment. The future is unknowable, so perhaps an even more seismic event will occur in the near future – although other than a world war, it is hard to think of one. To gain a better sense of how the spread of COVID-19 fits into a historical context, I recently interviewed two former CEOs of major global companies who also sit on the boards of other global firms, both aged over seventy-five, and my colleague Henry Mintzberg, who is in the same age group. I wanted to get the perspective of people who had seen and done a lot in their long and well-lived lives. When I asked them if today's crisis was unique, they all agreed that it was. It seems that you have to go back to the Second World War to find another period of similar tumult.

It appears inevitable that, at a minimum, we are headed toward a time of problems with value chains supplying the things we have become used to finding on retail shelves, real or virtual. After a time of uncertainty early in the pandemic, we are now back to a war for talent that famed management consultants McKinsey & Company have been talking about since 1997.[2] In 2021 and 2022, CEOs visiting our CEO Insights course for McGill University MBAs actively recruited our students after class was over. Restaurant owners in our neighbourhood ask me if I know of any students who want to work as servers, something they have never done before; post-pandemic, they are all looking for staff. As I write this in early 2023, the spectre of a recession is a reality; we will see where it goes.

I am a boomer who has taught at the universities of Oxford and Cambridge and at McGill University during the past twenty years. I've interviewed and worked with Generation Zers for my radio show, *The CEO Series*; travelled with them abroad to explore fast-growing economies with Hot Cities of the World Tour (year twelve coming up); and supervised their graduate theses and projects. Prior to joining the academic world, I spent eleven years working at IBM and Hitachi Data Systems. Thus, I have had the great fortune of spending much more time than the average boomer working alongside this generation – a generation that I very much appreciate and respect.

This book begins by explaining the worldview of Postmoderns to help you understand why Millennials/Generation Zers think the way they do. With this under our belts, I then share in the next five relatively short chapters some practical advice on how to work with them more effectively. Beyond coming to understand their worldview, I have conducted 800-plus interviews with under-thirty-year-olds across Canada, the United States, Japan, Iceland, the United Kingdom, and elsewhere. I have also interviewed 750-plus C-suite executives (executives with "C" in their titles, such as CFO, CMO, COO, etc. .) to get their perspectives on the joys and challenges of working with Millennials/Generation Zers.

As a professor, I have privileged access to undergrads not only in the classroom but also as part of my other activities. Most years, eight or so work for me as producers on my radio show, research assistants, or support organizers for our annual Hot Cities of the World Tour, so I spend many hours working closely with Zers. The tour, now in its twelfth year, is a twelve-day trip taking thirty McGill undergrads, a dozen alumni, and me to countries far from Canada – to Ghana and the Cote d'Ivoire in 2023. We have over thirty meals together, and it is a chance to have many in-depth conversations with Zers.

On the CEO side, I have a national radio show, *The CEO Series*, where each episode is my one-on-one interview with a CEO about their life and work, and a CEO Insights Class where three CEOS come to class in the fall – these give me access to senior people to get their perspective on working with Zers.

"The greatest danger in times of turbulence is not the turbulence: it is to act with yesterday's logic."
– Peter F. Drucker, management consultant and author

Generals Fight the Wars of Their Youth

We often hear from managers, "We are experienced leaders. Why should we change our approach?" General Martin Dempsey, chairman of the Joint Chiefs of Staff of the United States military under President Obama from 2011 until 2015, effectively explains why relearning and rethinking one's leadership management skills is essential.

Dempsey is a member of a rare group: he is one of only 214 people in American history to have been granted the rank of four-star general. Other individuals in this elite assembly include George Washington, Ulysses S. Grant, George S. Patton, and Dwight D. Eisenhower.

During an executive course that I taught at Duke University, General Dempsey shared a key lesson that he had acquired while in the military: "Generals fight the wars of their youth." He explained his statement by comparing his experiences as a young lieutenant tank commander to the experiences of today's military personnel. At the start of his career, he faced hundreds of Soviet tanks in East Germany (he had been trained to engage in massive tank battles, although thankfully he did not have to put this into practice at the time). The senior ranks that taught him about strategy had learned their most compelling lessons as pup lieutenants in the Vietnam War. As a general, his responsibilities naturally changed over time. He commanded active-duty troops fighting the Gulf War in Kuwait. The lessons he had learned from his lieutenant days, however, were mostly irrelevant to the war he was then fighting, and the lessons his commanders taught him from their days in Vietnam were even more outdated. Both were wars, yet they were extremely different. Both involved soldiers, yet soldiers had changed. Dempsey had to set aside what he had learned to command effectively under new and radically different conditions.

Executives and senior managers often face Dempsey's challenge. In their twenties and early thirties, they learn the art of management by watching their managers. This is particularly true for first-time managers. Underpinning this understanding of management is the worldview they acquired in university. To 'relearn' and 'rethink' as Dempsey did can be very difficult. While Dempsey had three wars as points of comparison to support his realization, managers rarely face the extreme conditions necessary for change. They generally stick to a comfortable management style, deviating only ever so slightly from it because that is what they know. What they know, however, is often not in alignment with the world of today. The lessons they cherish no longer fit with the reality of the Millennial/Gen Z workforce.

When I teach these ideas in the executive classroom, I give examples of three principles I learned in my twenties during my time at IBM that I have since had to throw overboard (summarized in figure 0.1).

The first jettisoned lesson, based on the principle that information is power, held that keeping information close to the chest granted the manager better control and, at times, the ability to manipulate others. In the world of Google and the Web, this lesson is largely irrelevant: employees have access to a staggering amount of information, and withholding information is largely impractical. In fact, undergraduates are often googling what their professors are saying in class. They readily raise their hands and point out the professor's errors – simply because they *can*. Moreover, in the wake of radical innovation with technology in the business sphere, managers are finding themselves in situations where precedent no longer holds, and they must look to those on the "front lines" of their business to remain competitive.

A second discarded lesson is that credentials matter. At one point in time, credentials were essential to many boomers. They represented professional credibility and gave considerable authority to those who possessed them – and the more, the better. Today, however, actual contribution matters much more, especially since a master's degree is the new bachelor's degree, such that in many firms, having a degree no longer makes you stand out.

Finally, the third abandoned lesson is the concept of who can be a leader. In the past, extroverts were considered to be the people who were going to be

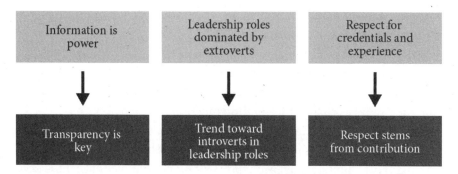

Figure 0.1
Examples of a shift in important principles between the 1980s and now

leaders. Scholars trace the rise of the extrovert model of leadership back to the 1920s when, at least in the United States, we moved from a culture of character to a culture of personality. Society favoured the person of action – articulate, quick on their feet – over the contemplative person. Recently, this trend has shifted.

Over the last decade, some of us who study leadership have focused on the leadership qualities of introverts. Susan Cain's excellent book, *Quiet*, has brought well-deserved attention to the topic. I have been conducting a research project in conjunction with Cain's Quiet Leadership Institute for four years, interviewing CEOs on the subject of introverts in the C-suite of large corporations. To our surprise (I am an extrovert), from 30 per cent to 35 per cent of C-suite executives happen to be introverts. Introverts (close to half the population) are increasingly recognized, as much as extroverts, as leaders. Another lesson to be tossed over the side!

Millennials/Generation Zers have, at times, a radically different perspective on how things should run and how they, as workers, should be worked with. I argue in this book that managers over the age of forty-five, also known as the Modern generation or Moderns, must adapt and change how they manage younger people, particularly those under the age of thirty-three (i.e., Postmoderns or Millennials/Generation Z – I generally refer to the individuals within this cohort as Millennials/Generation Zers in this book). The older generations must not fight the battles of their youth – those compelling lessons learned so long ago that have taken on the patina of truth in their minds. We must adjust our management approach to increase our effectiveness and work *with* our younger employees. The situation is not trivial; as Moderns once adopted a worldview different from that of their parents, so too have Millennials/Generation Zers. Worldviews have continued to evolve; many of the older generations have not kept up at the same rate as those of younger generations. Simply put: the world has changed, as they too must change.

Depending on life experience, education, and career, many older people find that they share much of the worldview of the Postmoderns. This realization is a very helpful starting place, though it is often hard to shake the lessons of our old world, the one we grew up in through our twenties and thirties.

To set the stage, chapter 1 outlines the importance of young people in organizations. As boomers retire, Millennials/Zers are increasingly filling the roles of middle manager and below in larger organizations, and in many start-ups, Millennials/Zers rule. Add to that the greater need for innovation in every industry. Change is no longer coming solely from the top, but increasingly from front-line troops and managers – in other words, increasingly from Millennials/Zers. In chapter 2, I describe the Modern worldview that people over forty-five were taught in their university education. Chapter 3 uses the evolution of medical practice as an example of Postmodern reasoning that I suspect we can all relate to, thus establishing a down-to-earth foundation for the definition of Postmodernism, which is discussed more fully in chapter 4.

While Postmodern thought extends to other topics, this book focuses primarily on what is relevant to management and leadership. We believe that the Millennial/Gen Z outlook involves contemporary perspectives on four important leadership issues:

- knowledge and truth – who has them and who controls them;
- hierarchy and its considerable decline;
- the way people relate to one another;
- the role of emotions in the workplace.

The final five chapters provide some of the necessary tools for leading, managing, and working with Millennials/Zers. Focusing on five key characteristics – listening, authenticity, purpose, reverse mentoring, and feedback – this book outlines strategic ways in which you can more effectively work with the Millennial/Z generations and unlock their potential.

The final chapter covers some material about Generation Zers and what they particularly bring to the workplace. They share much in common with Millennials but have some real differences as well.

I strongly believe that Generation Z can genuinely make an impact and significantly contribute to organizations. The challenge lies in unlocking that potential.

1

Young People
A Fundamental Shift in the Workplace

Young people are important (figure 1.1). Though this statement may seem self-evident, it has never been more relevant and requires the immediate and urgent attention of businesses. The population demographics of the developed world make this apparent: these countries' demographics display a simple, yet critical, pattern. Baby boomers and even some Xers are beginning to retire or, at least, step away from management roles.

There are too few young people in many countries, particularly in Europe, Japan, and increasingly in the United States and Canada (though immigration mitigates this a great deal in the latter two countries). In the United States, more than one-third of workers are now Millennials (people born between 1981 and 1996), and they recently surpassed Generation X as the largest contingent within the American workforce, according to a recent Pew Research Center analysis of US Census Bureau data.[1] As a result, a war for talent has been happening for a number of years and continues among businesses around the world.[2] The coronavirus crisis in 2020 appears, somewhat to our surprise, to have increased the war for talent.

The available workforce is primarily made up of young people. According to the UN Population Division there are 1.8 billion Millennials, which accounts for about a quarter of the world's population.[3] Thus, the ethos, social values, and beliefs of this generation will unquestionably come to dominate the workforce within the next decade. Senior leaders, therefore, will need to rethink the structure of their organizations in order to work with their future workforce effectively.

This book primarily focuses on the Western developed economies; however, we must realize that according to the *Financial Times*, emerging and devel-

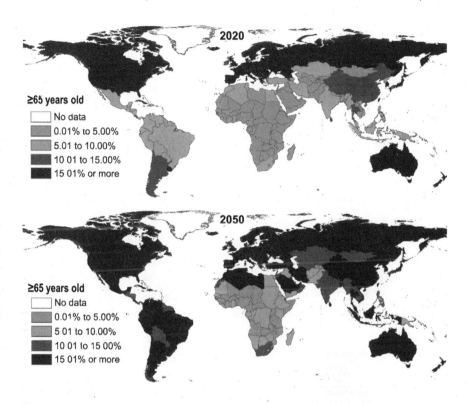

Figure 1.1
World demographic maps showing the proportion of the population aged 65 and over in 2020 and in 2050 demonstrating the speed at which populations are aging

oping economies are home to 86 per cent of Millennials.[4] The lives and careers of these Millennials/Zers are quite different in many emerging economies. As emerging-market multinationals enjoy greater success outside their home markets, they will inevitably experience the need to manage their Western colleagues. While perhaps not of great concern in their home markets today, understanding the younger workforce will be essential for successful international business engagements down the road. The shift in the workforce is universally relevant and must, therefore, be appreciated by business leaders regardless of geography or industry; however, the degree to which they have the Postmodern worldview will vary to some degree country by country, particularly in the emerging economies.

Today, unlike during most of human history, the workforce is simultaneously composed of several generations. Due to longer life spans, we now see
four (and sometimes even five) generations in the workplace. In 1900, the average life expectancy at birth was thirty-one years; in 1950, it was fifty;[5] and
in 2019 the UN gave the world average as being over seventy-two years.[6] This
is the first instance in history in which four generations are active in the workforce. In the past, people simply did not live long enough for this to occur,
and success only came after a long period of apprenticeship. Today, multiple
generations work side by side, presenting a tremendous range of ages in the
workplace, thus posing unique managerial issues.

This shift in workplace demographics has had a significant impact on workplace social dynamics and, ultimately, on the manner in which workplaces
operate. Figure 1.2 captures how the vast majority of organizations were run
in the 1980s. In the past, there was a clear hierarchy. Age mattered: people in
their thirties worked for people in their forties; they networked with peers in
their thirties and gave orders to people in their twenties. The importance of
age has since declined, particularly during the last decade, with both the elim-
ination of many middle management positions and the faster promotion of
high-potential youth.

These changes have reinvented the traditional pattern of what the typical
worker does and the age at which they do it. High achievers are spotted early
on and fast-tracked to senior-level roles, over their older colleagues who, sometimes, may have more experience. In addition, as innovative organizations
move away from "bureaucratic hierarchies" toward more integrated and multidisciplinary teams, conventional, tenure-based promotions no longer hold.

Two other factors have further muddled the traditional relationship between age and management responsibilities: retirement age and the rise of
technology. First, thanks to longer and healthier life spans, Baby Boomers are
changing the face of retirement, often working – at least part-time – beyond
the age of sixty-five. London Business School (lbs) professors Lynda Gratton
and Andrew Scott's 2016 book, *The 100-Year Life: Living and Working in an
Age of Longevity*,[7] makes a compelling argument that many will live and work
to a much older age than we have in the past. As this unfolds, age and management responsibility will be further decoupled.

In the best scenario, Baby Boomers will willingly relinquish their senior
management roles to younger people, while staying on and acting as advisers,

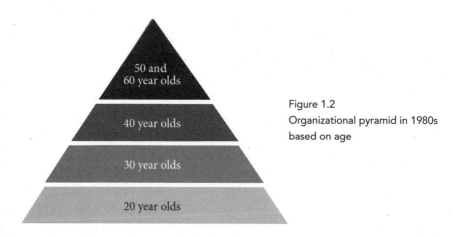

Figure 1.2
Organizational pyramid in 1980s
based on age

or moving on to less-demanding tasks. This allows businesses to embrace younger talent while conserving access to the expertise of their more experienced workers. More often, however, Boomers continue to occupy their higher-level roles, creating fewer growth opportunities for young and ambitious employees. Paying for Millennial children getting two or more degrees or who live at home till age thirty gets expensive.[8] Hence, up to four and certainly three generations are often coexisting in the workforce, sharing the spotlight, and sometimes fighting for dominance, or at least a significant voice.

The second muddling factor is technology, which has had a massive influence on knowledge acquisition. People can now connect to the information they need to do their job within seconds, any hour of the day. The Internet and social media have effectively put the Millennial way of thinking on steroids. Also, knowledge now ages much more rapidly than it has in the past. For example, in the field of psychology, psychologist Donald Hebb has estimated that the half-life of knowledge in his particular field is five years.[9] Bluntly put, if you graduated from university five years ago, your experience is somewhat out of date. If you graduated ten years ago, you are incredibly out of date. The mind shudders at the thought of having graduated thirty years ago! When I give speeches to executive audiences, I say to them, "the half-life of my wisdom is half of what it used to be and I am not as wise as someone who was my age twenty years ago." At first, they often look puzzled, but they tend to accept these ideas fairly readily. Though I do argue that I am still wise, I argue there is, as with intelligence, liquid wisdom and crystallized wisdom.

The concepts of liquid and crystallized intelligence were first proposed by psychologist Raymond B. Cattell in his book *Intelligence: Its Structure, Growth, and Action.*[10] He suggested that the ability to reason is fluid intelligence because it "has the 'fluid' quality of being directable to almost any problem." Crystallized intelligence refers to the knowledge you acquire through experience and education. With crystallized intelligence, you refer to your pre-existing knowledge: the facts, skills, and information you learned in school or from past experience. I would suggest that wisdom can also be viewed as fluid and crystallized: the former often more evident and strong among younger people with very fast minds, the latter evident in a trove of education, experience, and life expertise more typical of older people.

However, some lessons from my working for a decade at IBM are thirty years old and irrelevant in today's world, and some still have timeless value that I can share with my students. Even so, much of what I learned, both pure knowledge and wisdom, is no longer germane to today's turbulent world.

This further strains the conflict between generations in the workplace. The knowledge of younger generations, to them, feels (most often, rightfully) more relevant and valuable than the "dated" understanding of the older generation. To a considerable degree, we older people are just not as valuable as older people were thirty years ago when we were starting out.

Young people are often acutely aware of this. An excellent example is the now-typical interaction of a parent handing over their new electronic gadget to their teenager to learn how to use it. Generally speaking, children today seem to simply have an easier time grasping new technology. I once interviewed a twelve-year-old for my weekly *Forbes* blog; people were astonished when I told them that, until I added that she had 40,000-plus followers on TikTok. Social media provides another helpful example. Staying "connected" is incredibly important to the Postmodern generation; the connected lifestyle largely influences the way in which Millennials interact with one another and with their older counterparts. Generation Zers have this on steroids; in fact they are called the first truly digital generation.[11] Fewer face-to-face conversations are taking place, with business exchanges becoming increasingly impersonal and digital in nature. With more and more non-traditional companies (such as Google and Facebook) coming to the fore, skill and competency are quickly becoming more valued than age and seniority.

The divergence between these generations also manifests itself through their differing motivations. While Boomers and Gen Xers were, at times, more consumed by their careers, Millennials/Zers are typically more focused on better integration of their personal and professional worlds.[12] Personal development, self-empowerment, and quality of life are of greater importance. Many large com-

> "The[ir] expectations around work culture and lifestyle are higher. And I think that's really important. I believe they should be, and we should all be striving to have a better work-life balance."
>
> – Geoff Molson, CEO, Montreal Canadiens NHL Team

panies embrace their young workforce; they acknowledge the value of employing young people and fast-tracking their careers, while simultaneously allowing them to maintain work-life integration. Career development and personal development are more on par with each other, in part because some better organizations enable it. Young people only demand of their workplace what they know other organizations are providing. Now, start-ups are emerging that allow companies to outsource elements of their culture management, to better please Millennial/Gen Z workers. This indicates that "communicating" and "connecting" with this generation can be problematic for older people who may not understand the motivations and differing expectations of their young protégés.

The cumulative effects of these trends can be illustrated through the shifts in mentorship. Inverting the classical model of mentorship that most of us are accustomed to, it is now more and more common (as well as beneficial) for older people to be reverse mentored by their much younger employees. When I was growing up, mentoring was 98 per cent one-way. Today, I believe that I still mentor younger people about 75 per cent of the time, but 25 per cent, or more, of the time they are mentoring me – what I call reverse mentoring (more on this in chapter 8). The learning is much more symbiotic today than it was in the past. We discuss this further in subsequent chapters. In the same vein, large organizations are relying almost entirely on their younger generations for social media targeting and organizational strategy development; their skills are simply more relevant in the context of these roles. While older employees may possess an abundance of wisdom, judgment, and experience, young people are more capable of identifying what is relevant today.

The pace of change has always been rapid, but never more so than it is today. Moore's Law, named after Intel co-founder Gordon Moore, is an observation that the density of integrated circuit technology doubles approximately every two years. It has proven to be incredibly resilient since first being noted in 1965.[13] Another contributor to the rapid pace of change is the increase in the sheer amount of knowledge available to an ever-growing portion of humanity. The global economy has thus moved in the direction of a knowledge-driven economy, encouraging many nations, firms, and educational institutions to move into or at least toward the knowledge-production business. Unlike twenty years ago, knowledge has suddenly become available to everyone, and no generation has embraced this more than Millennials and Gen Z.

> " Millennials, more so than any previous generation, understand the importance of ideas. It is immediately obvious to them that they work in a knowledge economy."
> – John Micklethwait, editor-in-chief, Bloomberg News

This inevitably leads to the indisputable fact that young people are the future. While many companies are already embracing this realization, others are still hesitant. Contrary to the belief of some of these skeptical companies, working, moulding, and, most importantly, understanding Millennials/Gen Zers is not a hopeless challenge. In this book, I suggest that if we can understand the Modern and Postmodern worldviews, those of the Boomers/Gen Xers and Millennials/Gen Zers respectively, we will be much better positioned to understand (and be sympathetic to) how Millennials/Gen Zers want to be worked with. In the following chapters, we look at both worldviews, explore the similarities, and suggest ideas on how to bridge the gap between these generations and manage the many generational differences. The next chapter presents the Modern worldview, a necessary start to understanding the contrasting, and often conflicting, Postmodern worldview.

2

The Modern Worldview
Science, Architecture, and Religion

Who doesn't recall *The Jetsons*? At least, if you're over forty. The 1960s prime-time animated sitcom portrayed the future in very positive terms.[1] Families travelled via spaceships as opposed to cars; gleaming sky-high towers replaced individual houses; people worked three hours a day, three days a week. The world of the Jetsons supposedly provided the Baby Boomers with a glimpse into the future and the dream of a utopian, technologically advanced future.

The reality of the future that we experience today, however, is a far cry from that portrayed in *The Jetsons*. Most Americans work considerably longer hours than their parents. The ten-hour, six-day workweek is now considered the norm for many. Even before COVID-19, more and more people work from home, as commuting has become impractical, and the time spent commuting has steadily increased since 1980. In the 1960s, science and technology were expected to deliver technological innovations that would solve the world's problems and enable the creation of the Jetsons' utopia. For instance, while science has significantly extended the typical human lifespan, thereby addressing one of the Modern generation's most pressing issues, it has also introduced the combustion engine – a root cause of climate change, perhaps the biggest threat to humanity's future. While promoting and promising a future utopia to the Modern generation, *The Jetsons* failed to accurately depict our modern age.

> "The concept of nine-to-five is dead. You can always be contacted."
> – Brooke, manager, Monitor Deloitte (age 28)

Utopia (or lack thereof) aside, the Modern worldview has been shaped by the events and trends of the past few decades, with science and television acting as major contributors. The Modern worldview rejected much of its predecessors' worldview. Tradition was deemed foolish, too frequently based on superstitious thinking. Art, music, architecture, and politics were heavily debated.

One of the most significant departures from the past was criticism of the idea of God and religion. Perhaps the most famous cover of *Time* magazine, dated 8 April 1968, best expressed this paradigm shift with its title, "Is God Dead?" Indeed, in the late 1920s, British evolutionist and author Julian Huxley stated in his book *Religion Without Revelation* (republished in the 1950s):

> The supernatural is being swept out of the universe in the flood of new knowledge of what is natural. It will soon be as impossible for an intelligent, educated man or woman to believe in a god as it is now to believe the earth is flat ... or that death is always due to witchcraft ... The god hypothesis is no longer of any practical value for the interpretation or comprehension of nature, and indeed often stands in the way of better and truer interpretation. Operationally, God is beginning to resemble not a ruler but the last fading smile of a cosmic Cheshire cat.[2]

The intelligentsia of the time, which was primarily comprised of Moderns, devoured Huxley's words. Anti-religious beliefs dominated the academic world. God was seen as being a thing of the past. Religion seemed to be entering its final days. The Modern worldview challenged everything from the past. Baby boomers were indeed a rather lively lot.

This mindset, as with every mindset since the beginning of time, evolved gradually. Many of the drastic societal changes that were predicted never came to be. Religion, for example, survived. As two former writers for *The Economist*, John Micklethwait, a practising Catholic, and Adrian Woolridge, an atheist, argued, regardless of your personal view, God could not and would not fade away. On the contrary, Christianity remained

II "And the great prediction that was made when I was growing up and at university, that, as a society developed, religion would fall away, has proven to be wrong."[3]
– Tony Blair, former UK prime minister

quite strong in the United States and has since grown in many parts of Asia. Islam is another prime example of a religion that grew instead of flatlining.[4]

In a more concrete sense, the Modern mindset is clearly apparent in contemporary architectural trends. Architecture has also encountered a lot of

Figure 2.1
McLennan Library Building, McGill University, Montreal

"talk" and little "walk." Over the past couple of decades, executive programs at McGill University have taken place on the sixth floor of the Bronfman Building, overlooking a beautiful downtown campus at the base of a mountain. Scattered around the McGill campus are a variety of buildings. From the executive education classroom, you notice the beautiful Redpath Museum, built in 1882. The new Elizabeth Wirth Music Building, opened in 2005, is a stunning glass and metal edifice. Out of the corner of your eye, you notice a massive, grey, concrete Soviet-era-like structure. Dark and cold, the building is unwelcoming and, ironically, houses McGill's most extensive library. This begs the question, "What were architects thinking when they built this back in 1969?" The diversity in architectural styles seen across the McGill campus is a reminder that in architecture, as in many art forms, old approaches were at one point replaced by new, avant-garde styles.[5] Some proved to be lasting while others were – thankfully – abandoned.

Part of the zeitgeist of the Modern generation is the rejection of the past and the reinvention of the future. In understanding today's senior managers, who largely share this worldview, we need to appreciate the world in which these managers lived. Religion, architecture, and even their image of the future were all critically challenged. Tradition was thrown over, and every policy, subject, and approach came up for debate. By contrast, the workforce was one of the few stable environments. The hierarchical approach in the workplace remained static, consistent, and safe. The future hopes and desires envisioned by the boomer generation, similarly, either maintained their relevance or fell victim to the change in trends. The challenge in understanding the Modern worldview lies in clarifying what remains relevant and what has evolved.

In the next chapter, I define our understanding of the Postmodern worldview. This mindset is very different from the Modern worldview. Indeed, understanding what Postmodernism consists of is confusing since there are hundreds of different definitions of Postmodernism. Postmodernism "describes movements which both arise from, and react against or reject, trends in modernism."[6] This can apply to many facets of life; there is Postmodern architecture, art, Christianity,[7] dance,[8] literature,[9] music,[10] philosophy, psychology,[11] etc.[12] We are reminded of the sheer diversity of the term Postmodern by US Supreme Court Justice Potter Stewart's reference to pornography: "I can't define it, but I know it when I see it."[13]

You may note that this chapter is quite short. I have purposefully touched on only a few elements of the Modern worldview because many of you are likely a Modern, and no one knows the generation better than you do! For Millennials and Gen Z readers, hopefully this gives some sense of the worldview – albeit a fading one to some degree – of your elders. By highlighting specific examples, I have isolated the primary comparison points that are carried through to the next chapter. In order to understand Postmodernism, it is essential to first reflect upon how it conflicts and agrees with the Modern worldview.

More importantly, an understanding of the contrast between Postmodern and Modern worldviews is essential to gain an understanding of the inner workings of the younger workforce. The next chapter focuses on the profound changes that have occurred since the Modern age. The medical profession

Figure 2.2
Elizabeth Wirth Music Building, McGill University, Montreal

and medical practice serve as a microcosm of this evolving perspective because medicine has touched virtually every person and is an area to which most readers can easily relate.

3

Making It Real/Postmodernism Medicine
"Doc, I Have Three Theories about
What Is Wrong with Me"

When I was young, my mother would take me to the doctor for a medical appointment. Wearing a white lab coat with a stethoscope casually slung around his neck, he (at the time, the doctor was almost invariably a man) would conduct his examination and prescribe a treatment, if necessary. Most doctors were considered infallible experts whose diagnoses were not to be questioned; their place at the top of the social hierarchy was unassailable.

How things have changed! In the West, doctors are no longer considered infallible; in fact, many young people admire artists and financiers more than they do medical professionals. Doctors are now considered to simply be everyday, hard-working citizens. A visit to the doctor now entails, at the minimum, a short conversation; patients no longer sit in silence waiting for the doctor's verdict, before accepting it without question.

For example, Margaret, a Gen Z McGill student, typically researches her symptoms on Google, consults her father (who works in the pharmaceutical industry), and tests out a variety of pharmaceutical solutions on her own, prior to meeting with her doctor. She prepares herself well in advance for the patient-doctor dialogue because, in her words, "I don't want to sit in the waiting room for three hours unless I'm certain I need to see a doctor." In many ways, Margaret epitomizes the Millennial/Gen Z attitude toward medicine, a far cry from the Modern perspective that I experienced as a child. A doctor's word is no longer taken at face value. In essence, patients often challenge their doctor's verdict and even go on to seek additional consultations with other medical practitioners if they are not satisfied.

Moreover, apps and new technology continue to emerge that aim to eliminate visits to the doctor altogether – in line with the Millennial urge to avoid

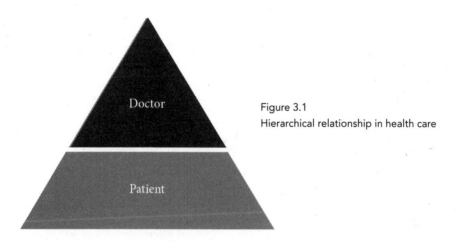

Figure 3.1
Hierarchical relationship in health care

this interaction. This is hardly a North American or European trend only; physician groups in Saudi Arabia, the UAE, and Thailand with whom I have spoken have often experienced similar patient interactions. This seems to be not so much a cultural nuance as a generational trend, seen most prominently with younger patients. In essence, patients are becoming "pseudo doctors" within a matter of hours of researching their affliction on the Internet, to the extent that it is not uncommon for patients to read the latest research findings in online medical journals long before their doctors do.

Millennials are as equally rebellious as Moderns; however, their interests lie in their desire for self-fulfillment, as opposed to achieving some greater good. While Moderns challenged broader social norms and issues – such as religion, politics, sexuality, and art – to bring about societal change, Millennials/Zers often choose to challenge societal problems such as climate change, racism, and inequality. Information is power, and with accessibility comes the confidence to use this information to one's own ends.

Margaret, for example, has faith in her WebMD and Google research when discussing her "what is wrong with me" theories with her doctor. When she does this, regardless of her doctor's comparatively superior medical education and experience, she does not feel that she is overstepping any bounds of propriety: if it concerns her well-being, she has a strong need to express her opinions.

Medicine is, therefore, an excellent place to consider Modern and Postmodern worldviews and attitudes in our everyday, practical world. Many changes, both scientific and social, have occurred in medicine over the past few decades. This has led to a shift in hierarchy – between the physician and the patient – with the medical profession's openness to more than one "truth" about how best to heal our bodies.

Alternative medicines are also becoming *de rigueur* for more and more people. Up to the 1980s, Western-trained physicians in white coats were the sole source of medical knowledge for the vast majority of the Western world. By contrast, today, more and more Westerners, especially Millennials, turn to online research as well as complementary and alternative medicine (CAM).

The National Centre for Complementary and Alternative Medicine defines CAM as "a group of diverse medical and healthcare systems, practices, and products that are not generally considered part of conventional medicine," a group that includes naturopathy, chiropractic manipulation, traditional Chinese medicine, meditation, yoga, and acupuncture. These terms have become increasingly well known in the Western world. In fact, as early as 2007, 38 per cent of people in the United States (more than one in three) used or had used some sort of complementary or alternative medicine. After I hurt my foot playing ice hockey, I ran into the father of a student of mine. He is an Ottawa-based anesthesiologist and suggested two courses of treatment for my foot: a bag of ice and a visit to an acupuncturist. This type of advice would have rarely been given ten years ago, let alone by a medical professional. Thus, as the medical profession has changed to accommodate and embrace the Postmodern worldview so too must managers.

This leads to two key questions: What causes these shifts? And what underlies the Millennial mindset?

The CAM Debate: Should We, Shouldn't We?

Consider the following scenario: Jane is in a state of shock – she has just been diagnosed with stage 3 breast cancer. Dr Smith has already outlined a recommended plan of treatment. Now Jane must face her stark reality and decide her next steps: Surgery? Chemotherapy? Radiation? The choice is hers, and she is feeling overwhelmed. Walking back to her car in the hospital parking lot, she suddenly recalls a television segment from a few months back. She remembers the announcers mentioning the use of alternative, non-traditional therapies. She approaches her oncologist about these options, and despite being met with skepticism, Jane decides to research and explore them on her own.

Jane's curiosity about the world of CAM practices is not unusual, especially among Millennials. Dr Saleem Razack, a pediatrician at Montreal Children's Hospital and assistant dean of admissions, equity, and diversity at McGill University School of Medicine,[1] has indicated that this is a visible trend: there has been an absolute explosion of interest in, and use of, alternative medicine in Western society. Dr Razack believes that in order to better understand the massive shift in acceptance of alternative therapies, one must look at the underlying changes in the sociology of medicine: what is lacking in modern medicine, and what are physicians not doing? He goes on – perhaps unsurprisingly given the Postmodern perspective – to describe the importance of a physician and patient forming a relationship of trust and confidence: "It's about the subject [patient] rather than the illness. We must look at the patients subjectively; something physicians fail to do." By "subjectively," Dr Razack means seeing a person holistically rather than through the traditional model of a semi-mechanical biological system.

The debate regarding traditional practices versus CAM practices resonates with our understanding of the contrast between Modernism and Postmodernism. While traditional methods are still incredibly important and relevant, we cannot ignore the increasing acceptance of CAM. With the evolution of medicine and technology, ordinary people outside of the traditional medical profession have gained a voice. Consequently, societal norms have shifted to embrace and adapt to these voices, which only encourages an increase in their number.

This change in medical perspectives can be tied to the broader trend – that Millennials/Zers base their thoughts and actions on a completely different mindset than that of their Modern predecessors. However, Moderns have themselves increasingly embraced these Postmodern attitudes toward medicine. If you asked a Modern, such as me, whether they would challenge their doctor's diagnosis using their personally prepared research, the answer would be a resounding "yes." This response stands in stark contrast to the long-gone image of doctors being infallible! Naturally, Moderns have come to adopt and appreciate these new approaches to medicine.

Why, then, would Moderns not also recognize the benefits of embracing Postmodern attitudes in the workforce? Why would they not at least attempt to understand the Millennial/Gen Z mindset, which would be the natural evolution of thinking about management issues? Why should the response to Postmodern thought in management be any different than the response to Postmodern thought in medicine?

Returning to Jane's predicament, we understand that she is aware of the success rate of conventional medicine. Still, she is afraid of the very unpleasant side effects that traditional cancer treatments entail. She is also concerned with the level of individual care that she will receive. Sadly, due to time and budget pressures on physicians, too many of them are perceived as overly calm and passive about patient care. Part of the appeal of CAM therapies is the optimistic view of their proponents. CAM practitioners invest significant time and energy into their patients' cases, lending a personal and human touch to their treatment. They empower their patients with encouraging words and the ability to make informed choices. CAM practitioners base their treatments on the belief that patients should be treated as individuals rather than as a constellation of symptoms.

Traditional physicians, on the other hand, argue that their practices are based on proven methodologies. They outline their higher success rates in the battle against cancer. They acknowledge that their bedside manners need improvement, and this issue is being addressed by the addition of classes on interpersonal communication in medical school programs. However, they strongly emphasize that their primary concern is the patient's well-being.

CAM practices are of concern to many traditional physicians. They are often horrified by the lack of quality control in some CAM practices. For example, they have indicated that, concerning dietary supplements, manufacturers "are not required to prove efficacy or safety of a product prior to marketing it. Supplement manufacturers are not obligated to report adverse events to the FDA."[2] Another concern is the lack of evidence associated with CAM approaches. Evidence-based medicine seeks to apply the rigorous scientific method to clinical decision-making to produce optimal, empirically observable, and statistically significant results. In evidence-based medicine, the gold standard is the placebo-controlled double-blind study, which is designed to eliminate any bias during the testing of a product.

Much of the skepticism of traditional physicians with CAM is the fact that their practitioners typically don't use the placebo-effect double-blind study. Dr Razack,[3] however, acknowledges the Millennial mindset and does not entirely discount the efficacy of alternative medicine. He maintains that "to judge whether something works or not, I still need the scientific method … But whether there is usefulness and truth in some of the alternate medicines, I believe there may be some in different places. I do not discount it, but it has to be proven. I am open-minded, but for me to incorporate it into the world of medicine, it has to be evaluated by the way we evaluate things."

The debate, therefore, continues. Both sides put forward valid arguments. What this debate illustrates, within the framework of this book, is that the medical profession has developed, and so must we as managers. Medicine is undoubtedly no more sophisticated or complex than management – after all, management deals with the complexity of the human mind, heart, and soul. The Millennial generation holds different standards and expectations with regard to their professional lives. Moderns must continue to embrace and adapt to these changes, as they have done in the medical context.

As we have seen with Jane, whether or not we belong to the Postmodern generation, we tend to be more willing to embrace change when faced with a dire situation. Jane is incredibly open-minded toward alternative diagnoses and treatments because her situation calls for it. We purposefully did not mention her age in order to demonstrate that it is not relevant. She could very well be a Modern who already embraces some aspects of Postmodernism (without even realizing it). Postmodernism is not as drastically different or life-changing as many Moderns think. In essence, they simply need to recognize the key factors of the Postmodern mindset and be open to the unique perspectives of this generation.

FAQ: **What about China, Russia, and India? Do They Have Postmoderns?**

II I have taught this material many times to executives in all three countries. The conclusion? India is the most Postmodern, followed by Russia and then China. And from talking to academics and students there, I would suggest that, increasingly, Postmoderns are the considerable majority. Ideas tend to cascade from one leading university to the next, eventually making their way into the broader society. Therefore, I believe that Postmodernism will be fully and globally embraced one day."

I presented these ideas a few years ago to an audience of about 300 physicians and nurses at a Saudi Arabian medical complex within the King Fahad Medical City. They agreed that the key elements of Postmodern medicine were already part of their clinical practice.

Patient-Doctor Dynamics in an Internet-Savvy World

The Millennial/Z generations have several unique characteristics that must be understood by Moderns in management if they are to manage them successfully. Again, I can use medicine and the patient-doctor dynamic as an analogy to the shift in mindset that must be understood to accommodate the Postmodern worldview in the workplace.

According to the National Cancer Institute's Health Information National Trends Survey, in 2020, 72 per cent of Americans searched online for health information,[4] up from 61 per cent in 2009[5] and only 25 per cent in 2000.[6] The widespread availability of information, particularly the explosion of health websites, has created more knowledgeable and demanding patients. Of the online searchers, an astounding 60 per cent thought the information they found online was as credible and effective as the medical information they received from their doctor, if not more so.[7] A large number of articles and studies have evaluated the transformed patient-doctor dynamic. One key trend that has emerged is the increasing number of "e-patients" who research their symptoms, consider multiple sources of readily accessible information, and partake in the decision-making process. Compared with the passive patients of twenty years ago, the e-patient is extremely familiar with their body and, most importantly, doesn't shy away from questioning or challenging their physician's diagnoses.

The shift in patient mentality from passive recipient to active contributor has reshaped the patient-physician dynamic. The traditional "paternalistic" model of patient care has been rejected and replaced by a new "participatory" model.[8] McGill University's former dean of medicine, Dr Richard Levin, recounts the style of medicine that existed in his first years as a doctor in the 1960s: "It was an era of paternalism, there was a strong belief that patients had to trust completely what the doctor said without question, that was the process of healing and doctors felt no compunction about giving full disclosure to patients."[9] With the arrival of the Internet, doctors suddenly became unsure as to whether access to more health information would be detrimental, as opposed to beneficial, to a patient's health. They were, and to some degree remain, apprehensive of addressing patients armed with information. Not only do they have to explain in detail their diagnoses but also they are expected to provide an array of alternative treatments. Interestingly, younger, Internet-savvy doctors have been more accepting of a new collaborative approach. The less technologically oriented Modern doctors felt that this new trend in the availability of information was threatening their authority.

In other words, the Postmodern physician has accepted (and embraces) the inevitable change caused by the Millennial/Z generation's worldview and consequently has adapted their practice to accommodate these changes. These physicians have relinquished their old ways and met their patients' evolving needs. They understand the meaning of the new patient-doctor relationship and make themselves relevant. With knowledge comes power – it is an incontrovertible fact that patients are no longer limited to relying solely on the advice of their family physicians. For the most part, they are free to consult whomever, whenever. As a result, those in the medical field are increasingly being told to adopt a business-like marketing relationship with patients since they are easy to acquire but hard to keep. Patient care needs to be personalized and accommodating, or retention becomes extremely difficult. If doctors are archaic and stubborn in their practices, they will inevitably experience a loss in patients.

Management is no different. The Millennial/Z generations want to work for corporations that are willing to evolve and change every few years. Upper management that continues to have a "dinosaur" mentality will only alienate these workers and increase the turnover rate among younger employees, similar to the poor patient retention of physicians who are reluctant to change. Millennials/Zers are uninterested in wasting their time; if they sense resistance to change, they will leave.

"Millennials are more demanding on their employer to provide them opportunities to grow. And if they find that they're stagnating and they're not being challenged, they will leave."
– Mark Hantho, chairman, Global Capital Markets, Deutsche Bank AG

What Are Your Values?

The Postmodern world is characterized by a change in social values, including:

- privileging the individual voice;
- focusing on emotions;
- demanding personalized attention;
- rethinking wellness;
- searching for variety over universal options.

It is crucial that Modern managers clearly define their values to accommodate and reflect these newly established social values.

To illustrate how the medical profession has accommodated these five values, I would like to introduce our next case: Charles, a surgical consultant by profession, can relate to the Postmodern change in social values, and he witnesses the weakening impact of his medical advice on a daily basis. The root cause is the loss of faith by patients in the medical system's effectiveness. Countless times, he has heard his colleagues recount stories of their patients' demands for more "plausible solutions." Though challenged, Charles, unlike his colleagues, understands that he can still be a respected physician within the Postmodern environment by adapting and changing his societal outlook. He began his adaptation by acknowledging that every patient has a unique voice, no matter their age, race, gender, or profession.

The Postmodern generation's placing of a higher premium on emotions than previous generations translates into a comprehensive view of the world involving more open communication and acknowledgement of others' feelings. This shift has also transformed the medical profession, specifically in regard to medical education. As detailed in the *Journal of American Medical Colleges*: "Medical education must change to meet the health care needs of the population and the changing demands of patients ... medical schools must increase their emphasis on primary care, as well as improve the overall competency of medical students in the interpersonal dimension of practicing medicine."[10] This "in touch" development is reflective of Postmodern values and has fundamentally influenced both physician-patient interaction and medical education curricula. Namely, North American medical colleges have now begun to prominently feature courses in communication skills and require an empathy assessment as part of admission requirements. This is also a part of rethinking wellness – what it means to be well, going beyond the body and including the spirit and mind side of things – something that particularly came to the fore during and following the COVID-19 pandemic.

Moreover, Millennials/Zers have greater expectations for individual and personalized attention. The desire for health care suited to personal needs has been amplified. An excellent example is pharmacogenetics, the study of genetic differences in metabolic pathways that affect individual responses to drugs, which will likely revolutionize the pharmaceutical market in the next few decades. This novel approach aims to customize treatment options for cancer patients, among others. In conjunction with the focus on individual attention, the number of doctors specializing in a specific area of medicine is increasing. The combination of these two trends will enable patients to fully personalize their health care to their liking.

> "The real role of a physician, [which] we're trying to teach our medical students, is how to interpret the knowledge in the context of the individual who sits before you. Hence, you should practise skills like listening as opposed to talking, and skills like observation instead of action."
> – David Eidelman, dean of medicine, McGill University

Finally, Millennials/Zers are interested in all possible alternatives; they dislike the idea of following a predetermined protocol. This increased interest in variety, as opposed to a single universal option, has caught the medical profession by storm. As before: knowledge is power. Cancer is not necessarily a death sentence – radical alternative treatments are being developed every day. Information flows faster than it can be absorbed, and Millennials stay more informed than their Modern counterparts. In a sense, they can be considered risk-takers and early adopters – perhaps even adventurers who are ahead of the game. Millennials are intrigued by therapies that will work for them and that are designed for the unique individual. A doctor's goal, meanwhile, is to simply treat the patient. A happy medium between the two would entail a doctor understanding, acknowledging, and appreciating a patient's worldview (though not necessarily fully accepting it) and working alongside the individual as much as possible.

Realizing this happy medium is essential toward effectively managing Postmoderns in the workplace. As noted above, the practice of medicine is not altogether different from that of management in any organization. Changes

"I have taken the time to understand my health, and so, when I step into a doctor's office, I expect my opinions to be taken seriously and to have an open dialogue with the medical professional."
– John Martin, BSc student, Queen's University (age 21)

have occurred in the workplace, and as in the medical context, they are impossible to ignore. To successfully carry out their duties, managers, like doctors, must come to terms with the shifts in the workplace and actively work with their Millennial/Gen Z colleagues. By gaining an understanding of Postmodern expectations and adapting to them, doctors have been able to address their patients' needs and, many times, save their lives. While doctors may not necessarily agree with the many complexities of the Postmodern worldview, they cannot afford to disregard it. Similarly, managers cannot afford to overlook the perspective Millennials/Zers bring to the workplace. The next chapter focuses on outlining

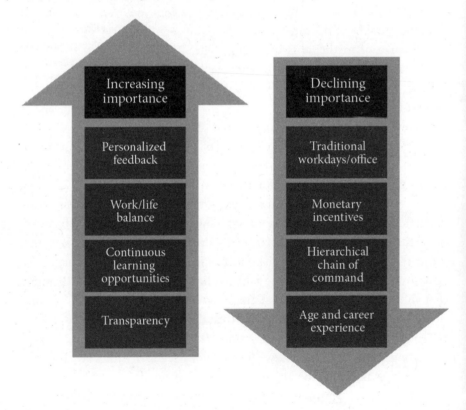

Figure 3.2

Changing values and impact on workplace expectations and operations the Postmodern worldview in more detail, enabling a greater recognition of the perspective for the Modern audience for whom this is so critical in the workplace.

This chapter was written with the help of Dr Avigyle Grunbaum, Dr Anais Hausvater, and Dr Mali Worme, graduates of the MD program, McGill University, Faculty of Medicine, and former research assistants of mine.

"Millennials have different priorities. Their priorities aren't necessarily having a stable job for forty years and putting all their strength into that. I think that they have a more balanced outlook on life, and that tends toward having people in medicine who might not be working as long hours or who might not be working the same profession in the same place for forty years."
– Dr Daniel Borsuk, chief, associate professor of plastic surgery, Oral and Maxillofacial Surgery, Université de Montréal

4

The Postmodern Worldview
Truth, Emotions, and Hierarchy

The Postmodern worldview is a rich and complex topic. For the purposes of this book, I focus on four aspects of Postmodern thought. Though they overlap to some degree, they are the most relevant to management and leadership of your Millennial/Gen Z workforce:

- the changing nature of truth;
- who interprets knowledge and truth;
- the importance of emotions;
- the declining importance of hierarchy.

The Changing Nature of Truth

In the 1950s and early 1960s, most members of society seemed to – for the most part – agree on the concepts of "right" and "wrong." The end of the 1960s, however, quickly saw those ideas challenged with the "update" of universally accepted "Truth." The combination of the controversial Vietnam War and other examples of belligerence overseas, the shocking treatment of many African Americans, and the idea that we needed and deserved an equal and free society brought about massive civil unrest. With no other sources of information, the truth was seen as what the government and media had spoon-fed people. It was accepted at face value, with little or no criticism.

Daniel Levitin,[1] a James McGill Professor Emeritus of the Psychology of Electronic Communications, captures the Postmodern view of truth as artists and scientists see it in the introduction of his book *This Is Your Brain on Music.*

The work of artists and scientists is ultimately the pursuit of truth, but members of both camps understand that truth by its very nature is con- textual and changeable. Dependent on the point of view, and that today's truths become tomorrow's disproven hypotheses or forgotten "objets d'art." One needs look no further than Piaget, Freud, and Skinner to find theories that once held widespread currency and were later overturned (or at least dramatically re-evaluated). In music, a number of groups were prematurely held up as of lasting importance: Cheap Trick were hailed as the new Beatles, and at one time the *Rolling Stone Encyclopedia of Rock & Roll* devoted as much space to Adam and the Ants as they did to U2. For the artist, the goal of the painting or musical composition is not to convey literal truth … For the scientist, the goal of theory is to convey "truth for now" – to replace an old truth, while accepting that someday this theory, too, will be replaced by a new "truth," because that is the way science advances.[2]

Let's hear from today's politics.[3] In late 2016 Steve Schmidt, an American campaign strategist and public relations worker for the US Republican Party, gave a talk in Montreal.[4] What he said reflected today's view of truth for many. "Truth and reality have become subjective. Donald Trump has demonstrated that again and again in the 2016 campaign." Schmidt was the senior campaign strategist and adviser to the 2008 presidential campaign of Senator John Mc-Cain and is very knowledgeable about American politics. As in art, truth in politics has changed. Former president Trump took this to new heights;[5] during the Trump years, the *New York Times* regularly published articles questioning the veracity of many of President Trump's public statements. In the Trump era we often heard that we were living in a post-truth world.

Millennials/Zers are far more skeptical about truth. Their virtual world enables both extreme distortion and exposure. To them, the truth is variable, continually shifting, and affected by "media bias." In today's world, many will only pay attention to what agrees with them; in the 1960s and '70s, a world of three major television networks in the United States, you could not do this. Absolute Truth (with a capital "T") is a rare sight nowadays, even more so than it was twenty or thirty years ago. Increased access to information delivered a single, uniform Truth in the 1950s and 1960s, but it also led to its distortion and deterioration.

> "The Millennial cohort is generally not as willing to just accept what is given to them. They are sceptical since they have grown up in a world where they can independently seek answers on Google and social media."
> – Brian Fetherstonhaugh, worldwide chief talent officer, Ogilvy Group

The positives and negatives of society's embrace of a universal Truth found a clear counterpoint with the acceptance of tolerance and pluralism in more recent decades. No longer was a universal Truth seen as the norm, but rather, multiple (and shifting) truths were adopted throughout society. Diversity, for example, was and continues to be a predominant theme that stemmed from the evolution of Truth after the civil rights movement in the United States and the introduction of the concept of multiculturalism with the Charter of Rights and Freedoms in Canada. Diversity would not have been embraced had the nature of Truth not changed. All of this to say, in contemporary society, what is accepted as truth is continuously evolving and changing as social norms and values evolve. There is no longer one single, universal Truth.

Oxford Dictionaries declared its 2016 Word of the Year to be "post-truth" after it saw a 2,000 per cent increase in usage. Oxford defines it as "relating to or denoting circumstances in which objective facts are less influential in shaping public opinion than appeals to emotion and personal belief." We can attribute its recent surge to the sort of anti-establishment and emotion-driven politics that gave rise to the election of President Trump and the Brexit decision. That being said, the post-truth world that we find ourselves in is the result of more significant phenomena. Philosopher and author Professor A.C. Grayling blames the rise of social media and the growth of income inequality since the 2008 financial crisis for a society where opinions and feelings matter more than facts. On the one hand, when people feel shortchanged by the system, they are more susceptible to reactionary thinking. On the

> "All my analyses are against the idea of universal necessities in human experience. Such necessities must be swept aside as baggage from the past: It is meaningless to speak in the name of – or against Reason, Truth or Knowledge."
> – Michel Foucault, French philosopher and historian, 1993

other hand, the constant barrage of information and opinions from the Internet not only disorients but also makes it difficult to discern what is news from what is opinion. Too many of us live in an echo chamber!

According to a 2022 Gallup poll, Americans' trust in mass media has fallen to an all-time low, with only 34 per cent indicating they have at least a "fair amount of trust in the media." Public distrust makes sense when one considers the Postmodern worldview. Why should people accept what they are told by mainstream sources when they already have direct access to the "real" world through the user-generated content that permeates their online media? We have the ability at our fingertips to find evidence or opinions supporting any and all narratives, so why would we want to accept universal Truths or "facts," especially those that upset us? As frightening as a post-truth world may appear, Millennials/Zers may be the key to living and succeeding in it.

Millennials/Zers are pioneers in sorting through what seemed to be universal Truth and their individualized, subjective concept of truth.[6] They thrive on information and can be fanatically analytical. They are aware of the fine line between the two varieties of truth, yet they often flirt with the frontier between the two. Their sense of right and wrong differs significantly from that of a Modern. They often justify their actions based on their understanding of the truth. In the mind of the Millennial/Zer, truth is obtained through access to information.

"Going online means I see a mix of news and comments, opinions, and stories. Finding truth in it all is a tough task. That's why my colleagues and I regard 'trust' as something built on an individual basis, based on personal relationships."
– Vikrum Papa, College of Business graduate, University of Illinois (age 22)

Who Interprets Knowledge and Truth

As we saw in the previous chapter, in which I used the example of the evolution of Postmodern medicine, the holder of truth and knowledge has changed. The authorities no longer possess absolute control over access to information. In grade ten, I wrote a term paper on Shakespeare's play *Macbeth*. It was returned to me with a giant red "X" across the whole first page. According to my teacher, my interpretation was wrong. Today, when I share this story with my undergraduate students, they react in horror at the thought of the intellectual assault they suppose I must have experienced. In their opinion, my perception could not have been incorrect. At best, it was different from the traditional interpretations of the play, which might be better, but certainly not wrong.

During my high school days, there was only one perception of how the oeuvre of Shakespeare was meant to be interpreted. Deviation from this classical perception was unacceptable and was simply considered to be wrong. The focus was on Shakespeare and the meaning of his words as defined by him; it did not matter what the reader subjectively experienced when reading the author's work. Postmodern interpretation of the same literature, however, has since shifted gears, now placing that interpretation in the eye of the beholder and channelling the reader's perception. Nobel Prize candidate and esteemed author Milorad Pavi expresses this change by explaining that "we have always talked of talented or gifted writers; we should talk of gifted and talented readers."[7] Although this statement can be considered extreme, it does demonstrate a shift in focus: away from the expression of the writer and toward the interpretation of the reader.

This trend is a unique characteristic of the Postmodern world and can be seen to stem from many diverse factors. In March 2012, Britain's *Guardian* newspaper interviewed writer Ian McEwan,[8] who described an interesting story wherein his son's teacher had disagreed with the interpretation he had presented in his A-level essay on his father's novel *Enduring Love*. This amusing yet poignant incident demonstrates that interpretation varies from person to person, and that the original intended message of the content is less important, even to its author. No single interpretation can be considered right or wrong. In the Postmodern context, they are all "correct" because they are based on each individual's subjective experience.

With such easy access to information, knowledge is equally accessible, for the most part, to most individuals. The beholder, however, is unique. The author has ceased to be the dominant force; the reader is the critical actor. They are the interpreter and user of the information.

Knowledge creators, like the doctors of the previous chapter, have adapted to this Postmodern trend and can no longer assume that they are catering to a homogeneous audience. Instead, they acknowledge that the knowledge they impart must cater to Millennials/Zers who are profoundly shaped by their life experiences, and who will see what they want to see in any text.

The Privileging of Emotions

Having an emotional moment at work? Time for a coffee break! I can recall during my days at IBM that anytime someone got emotional, the team would take a coffee break to allow people to "calm down," before then collectively dealing with the problem at hand. The situation was handled by ignoring the conflict and sweeping any recollection of it under the boardroom table. Emotional outbursts were discouraged.

Older readers might remember Sergeant

"My friends and I read many different stories across many different platforms on a daily basis. We don't place much emphasis on the author or source; however, we do care about our own reaction, feelings, and opinions on the subject. After all, we trust the people we know more than somebody on the Internet or TV that we've never met."
– Alexandra Breukels, consultant, EY Vancouver (age 23)

Friday's line from *Dragnet*, "Just the facts, ma'am, just the facts." That rational, emotionally detached approach was deemed the most effective method for dealing with problems. Pure thought, however – à la Mr Spock in the 1960s cult television series *Star Trek* – fell sadly short of effectively resolving conflict in the workplace. In the intervening years, emotions were more fully introduced into the workplace and gained momentum. For Millennials/Zers, facts and emotions are almost on par with each other.[9]

Professor Gianpiero Petriglieri at INSEAD (a top European business school), who is also a medical doctor with a specialization in psychiatry and who has practised as a psychotherapist, eloquently encapsulated this trend in a *Harvard Business Review* article: "Hardly a day goes by that I don't meet it, the struggle with emotions at work. The misunderstood colleague, filled with frustration, attempting not to show it; the executive wondering how to confront her team's lack of enthusiasm; the student hesitating to confess his affection to a classmate."[10]

This appreciation of emotions has, therefore, become increasingly important in the context of management. As Petriglieri has pointed out, two decades have passed since emotional intelligence became a part of conversations between, and evaluations of, executives and managers. Yet he argues, "We remain unsure about what to do with emotions at work."[11] I believe it is the older Modern executives who remain unsure about the place of emotions in the workplace because of their worldview. Millennials/Zers are less uncertain.

With an appreciation of a quantitative measurement of emotional intelligence, or the emotional quotient, Petriglieri argues that "We have come to regard emotions as assets – precious or toxic as they may be – rather than simply data. Therefore, we focus on managing them, which often means trying to exploit, diffuse, or sanitize them, far more than staying with them long enough to discern their meaning. And when we do the latter, we usually interpret them as revealing something about their owners alone."[12] To accommodate and motivate Millennials/Zers, managers must go beyond this attitude of simply managing emotions and move toward accepting them as a necessary and legitimate part of managing and interacting with their younger employees.

In the last decade or so, there has been a growing interest in the idea of a person being able to increase their charisma. Books that seem among the more research-based (and sensible) include *The Charisma Myth* by Olivia Fox Cabane[13] and *Power Cues: The Subtle Science of Leading Groups, Persuading Others, and Maximizing Your Personal Impact* by Nick Morgan. This reflects the trend of greater appreciation of emotions in the workplace.[14]

Rather than just the "big brain" that can analyze problems to the nth degree and come up with the "perfect solution" on the fly, leaders today, perhaps more than in the past, are recognized as needing the ability to inspire others and help them deliver on the implementation of an idea. Mike Roach,[15] the CEO of CGI, a global IT outsourcer, while speaking in McGill's CEO Insights class for MBAS, appropriately stated that "strategy without execution is hallucination." Strategy and leadership, for the Millennial/Zer, can be more appropriately defined as the ability to bring a dream or vision to reality,[16] and emotions are central to delivering on our vision for all of us.

Of course, this "soft" approach with a strong emphasis on emotions is not entirely new. Looking back through military history, we note that soldiers were willing to die for their comrades, their superiors, and even their country's interests and societal values. A level of extreme bonding occurred, bringing fighting units together in combat. There was an outpouring of emotions, and in one of the harshest job environments at that. A memorable Hollywood scene that depicts the importance of emotion in this context takes place in the movie *Braveheart*. Mel Gibson's character, William Wallace – a commoner – unites thirteenth-century Scots in their attempt to overthrow the English ruling class. Wallace, with his face covered in blue war paint, gives a rousing speech, inspiring his troops to head into battle. The penultimate line of his address, "they may take our lives, but they will never take our freedom," captures the emotional resonance and depth of this scene. While many soldiers die, it is the emotion in the scene that gives their death meaning and engages the audience.

Millennials/Zers relate to the scene in *Braveheart* because they value emotion. They do not rely on or interpret information solely based on rational thought. An example is Postmodern architecture, which reflects the acknowledgement of emotion. Architects "give people buildings that look the way they feel."[17] If a company desires to project a relaxed, welcoming feeling, their building will likely be open and airy, with many windows and communal spaces. The workplace environment painstakingly caters to employees' needs. Postmodern literature is very similar – there is a need for emotional engagement. For literature intended to be appreciated and consumed by Millennials/Zers, publications tend to be free-flowing and whimsical, creating a powerful emotional connection with the reader.

The effect of emotion on people's lives and on society is not new. Rather, it is the public acceptance and acknowledgement that has come out of the woodwork. Interestingly, general research practices have begun to use emotion in their studies, as opposed to treating it as being immeasurable. The Postmodern generation trusts emotional context. They reject the sole use of mechanical and impersonal rationality of thought. They seek to understand the world on a deeper level.

The business world is no exception. With the recognition that emotions impact the workplace, their inclusion as a work consideration has seen enormous growth over the past two decades. The annual Academy of Management conference held each August is the world's largest gathering of business professors and doctoral students in business. For the past decade, one of the single most important topics – in terms of research presentations – has been "emotions in organizations." This topic has caught the interest of many management publications such as *Fortune, Forbes*, and *Harvard Business Review*, all of which have devoted articles to the discussion of emotions in the workplace. Workplace emotions have taken precedence when evaluating workplace productivity, employee loyalty, and job satisfaction.

The Postmodern generation believes that organizations can grow and prosper through emotional openness. They also perceive negative emotions as having the ability to destroy a company. They believe that emotions are as, if not more, important than rational thought. In her seminal work, *The Managed Heart*,[18] Arlie Hochschild studies the effects of emotional labour and the negative impacts of repressed emotions. Hochschild identifies "emotional labour" as the act of managing one's own emotions in the workplace.[19] Numerous studies have documented that a high degree of emotional labour can lead to burnout, employee dissatisfaction, and reduced productivity.

Postmoderns expect the challenges of emotional labour to be addressed, as they believe in the value of their own emotions in the workplace. I have students who, unhappy with their careers after graduating, openly express their disappointment to their managers to improve their working conditions. Feeling that their actions are both rational and reasonable, at no point did they feel their emotional expressions were inappropriate. They were taught that emotional intelligence supports innovation and creativity.

Utilizing emotional intelligence directly relates to strong leadership and teamwork. Postmoderns want to be able to express themselves. They want to be honest about their feelings and concise when discussing their views. Most importantly, they want to be heard. In response, companies have placed a renewed focus on managing the culture of their organizations, putting culture at the forefront of their management priorities.

> "When I look at Millennials, what I think they want most is to be heard and to make a difference."
> – Mark Parent, president and CEO, CAE

Quy Huy, a professor at INSEAD, has put forward the model "Five Emotional Levers" for today's leaders, which outlines the five most critical emotions in the workplace:

- respectful authenticity;
- deserved pride;
- realistic hope;
- aspirational discontent;
- thoughtful passion.

Huy makes the point that a very significant number of employees are not bringing their best to work. Two key dimensions he looks at are focus and energy. Management's job is to help employees see what they should focus on, and with Millennials/Zers in particular the "why" must be clearly explained.[20] The positive of explaining why with these generations is, firstly, it elucidates what is required, and secondly, they can debate with the why and often can help co-create with management a better strategy or approach to an issue. The dimension of energy is the main point of his Five Emotional Levers model. His research suggests that high-energy people are critical to the kind of innovation that organizations need to solve their pressing issues. How do you get people from low to higher energy? A key path is by managing and working with emotions. Though in a different way than Daniel Goleman's emotional intelligence, which is what an individual has. Huy argues that a manager or leader should manage the group emotions in order to get better performance from a group, particularly in times of change. In times of change, we human beings tend to be a bit like a deer caught in the headlights of a car: most of us stand stock-still, not moving. But during times of change we need to be particularly agile.

Huy suggests that managers and leaders should specifically focus on these five key emotional levers, give considerable thought to them, and develop specific actions to actively manage the emotions of their team (you read that right). This goes beyond "warm and fuzzy" feelings to concrete steps, particularly in times of change. What Huy is suggesting managers try to bring about is a collective emotional engagement, or group-level emotion. It is not about only managing the emotions of an individual but doing it for a team, and in the case of executives, for a large group of people. In a Postmodern world where emotions are on the same plane as thought, this is a particularly relevant and valuable idea.

Let me briefly review the five levers (for more details, please see the endnote citations to Huy's work).[21] *Respectful authenticity* means aligning your thoughts, actions, and feelings, effectively opening yourself up to constructive criticism. *Deserved pride* is essentially demonstrating an appreciation for people's differences and contributions. Pride is essential for us to rally around hard work, and because of the importance of the organization, it is worth sacrificing any reaction to it we might feel. *Realistic hope* is an inspiring feeling that actions today will improve the collective future. We may sometimes sacrifice today to secure a brighter future as a result of our diligence. *Aspirational discontent* is the belief that it is possible to reach your highest potential along with a feeling

> "All employees, especially Millennials, need to be inspired by the organization's noble mission."
> – Marc Parent, president and CEO, CAE

of dissatisfaction associated with complacency; great organizations are always trying to improve, day in and day out. *Thoughtful passion* recognizes that it is important to feel a high level of personal engagement and passion when it comes to facing any sort of challenge. This holds particularly true when you are looking for greater innovation, and who isn't in this world of disruptive business models?

Together these levers are essential in developing the sort of emotional capital that organizations can use to inspire collective action and to positively influence people.

The Decline of Hierarchy

When I was younger, we addressed older people by their titles. Today, instead of the more formal Professor Moore, students call me Karl with ease. Even more audacious is the fact that these young people have direct technological access to the most influential minds of our society, titled or not.

> "When [Millennials] go to a company, they do not see org charts and hierarchy; they just see a network. I think ceos have had to adapt to that – this whole notion of 'I rank higher than you on the org chart, therefore you will do what I say' doesn't work anymore."[22]
> – Adam Bryant, columnist, Corner Suite, *New York Times*

Students tweet their hockey analyses to prolific tsn commentator @BobMcKenzie, and he often engages in friendly banter with them. Others chat online with British comedian, actor, and author @stephenfry, who regularly tweets, jokes, and interacts with his followers. Others also tweet with *Globe and Mail* journalist Jeffrey Simpson, who responds to their questions every week. During the last Canadian federal election, students submitted their debate questions via online video, while political leaders responded to them on national television: the expectations surrounding acceptable dialogue have changed since Postmoderns no longer quite get the relevance of hierarchy. New hires want to engage not only with their boss but also with their boss's boss – and their boss's boss's boss. And businesses are responding. Morgan Stanley, for example, has implemented a

Twitter page and an internal Facebook platform for their employees. Company-wide communication and collaboration are being praised. A former student of mine, Ramzi Kaiche, even mentioned that upon joining the banking world, the first thing he was told was that they were a "horizontal organization, unlike traditional banking." Millennials/Zers are disinterested in the old style of hierarchy, and businesses are adapting to ensure they still attract high-end talent. The six degrees of separation between a CEO and front-line employees is diminishing.

Companies such as Google are attracting the world's most celebrated young technical and business minds because of their wafer-thin hierarchy. As I saw during a recent lunch in the Googleplex dining hall, a rookie software engineer can mingle with a senior product manager; actual hierarchical boundaries are limited in number, and the levels within the organization are few. Microsoft, on the other hand – not that long ago – had six to twelve layers of middle managers, depending on the department. They operate in a conventionally structured environment – a junior analyst would not dare suggest any new ideas to a senior manager five levels above his pay grade. Your place in that company is very clear.

> "My goal is to work at a corporation with a more horizontal structure, one that is willing to reward young talent and initiative. I believe my own experiences and hard work give me something of value to offer regardless of my age."
>
> – Max Laurin, Trinity College student, University of Toronto (age 22)

Several years ago, Canada's Privy Council Office commissioned David Eaves, a public policy expert, to write a report on how the Canadian public service could improve recruitment and retention of its young people: his report primarily focused on hierarchy. Eaves believed that young, talented twenty-something-year-olds were disinterested in the idea of seeing their ideas struggle through the various levels of the chain of command. As John Ibbitson elaborated on in his 2008 book *Open & Shut*: "Why would they want to work in a place where everyone can't talk to everyone about anything? If they think they need to talk to the deputy minister, they want to be able to talk to the deputy minister. They don't do bureaucracy."[23]

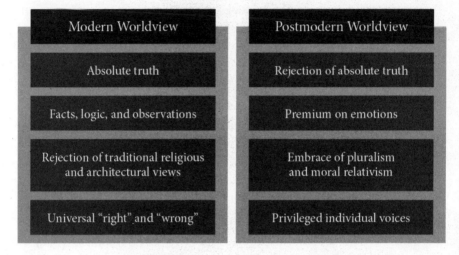

Figure 4.1
Brief snapshot of contrasting worldviews

Is There Post-Postmodernism?

Yes, there is. According to author Brian Kirby in *Philosophy Now Magazine*, "Postmodernism is dead and buried. In its place comes a new paradigm of authority and knowledge formed under the pressure of new technologies and contemporary social forces."[24] What it entails, though, remains to be defined.

Postmoderns disagree with the idea of overly close supervision. They believe that they will flourish without it. They somewhat understand the importance of having a boss, yet they do not feel that this should be limited to being a single individual. Postmodern mentality supports open communication amongst all employees. Even though you are the CEO, you are still an employee. That said, is there a time and place when hierarchy remains an appropriate approach? Yes! In times of crisis, most people find comfort in knowing that someone wiser is above them, making difficult decisions. Many Millennials/Zers expressed that they very much appreciated the CEO doing weekly video updates and town halls during the early days of the COVID crisis. When your house is on fire, you listen to the firefighter. You do not argue for a split second. These rigid hierarchical situations, however, are becoming fewer and fewer in number.

Five Ways to More Effectively Work with Postmoderns

We have now considered the Modern and Postmodern worldviews and, in our last chapter, looked at Postmodern medicine as a way to connect the more philosophical ideas of postmodernism to our everyday world. The next six chapters will provide tips on how to work more effectively with Postmoderns. We call this the "the Monday morning impact." The name derives from the critical question learned from my colleague Henry Mintzberg – that poses to managers: "What can we do, first thing Monday morning, that will have an impact?"

We hope you find your footing.

5

Privileging All Voices
Listen More, Talk Less

"The leader of the past knew how to tell. The leader of the future will know how to ask."[1]
– Peter Drucker, management consultant and author

Slow Down and Listen

Millennials/Zers firmly believe that their story, or their personal and subjective truth, is as good as anyone else's, regardless of their shortcomings in experience, age, or educational achievement. However, I argue that, contrary to popular belief, Millennials are not acting entitled, they are simply misunderstood. This is part of a larger characteristic of the Millennial/Z generations, which can be described as the death of meta-narratives and the rise of micro-narratives. Grasping this idea helps us understand why young people feel they must be heard.[2]

Meta-narratives are narratives about narratives of historical meaning that legitimize society by foreshadowing completion of an (as yet unrealized) master idea, i.e., they are broad, universal narratives that explain ideologies and world history. For just a few examples, think of communism during the Cold War, or free-market capitalism during the Reagan years. In the 1980s, the leadership of the developed world was primarily divided into two spheres of influence: the West led by the Americans and the East led by the Soviets, each spearheaded by their respective political classes in Washington and Moscow. The meta-narrative was that of capitalism versus communism as a means of organizing the economy.[3] However, with the fall of the Berlin Wall in 1989, communism largely ceased to be relevant.[4] It no longer exemplified the future evolution of social progress. Karl Marx's maxim, "from each according to his ability, to each according to his need," was no longer nearly as compelling as it had once been. True, it remained a principle in some parts of the world, but it no longer set the ideological narrative for a large portion of society. Free-market capitalism also met its comeuppance and slowly began to decline as the defining economic force in the West. Various economic systems emerged after the collapse of the Soviet Union, a sign that there was no longer one perfect way to run a successful economy. India, Sweden, and Canada all enjoyed considerable success despite having a market-oriented economy, socialist market economies, and mixed economies, respectively. In short, with the end of the Cold War and the collapse of the Berlin Wall, capitalism and communism ceased to be defining societal ideologies – and, consequently, the meta-narrative shifted.[5]

The Postmodern worldview does not rely on sweeping meta-narratives, but rather on individualized micro-narratives. *Micro-narratives* are small, local stories that are based on human experiences. These stories, and the truths that they embody, are derived from lived experiences and are greatly influenced by environmental and social contexts. The result is an individualized knowledge base that Millennials/Zers deem equally as valuable and valid as anyone else's – including, for our purposes, that of their superiors in the workplace. Given the ease with which Millennials/Zers can access information, the acquisition of knowledge itself has likewise become facilitated (for the most part). All that remains unique within this paradigm is the acquirer of knowledge, the person at the centre of this process. This results in the existence of "a multiplicity of theoretical standpoints," underscored by the idea that one's lived experience often cannot be accurately assessed against another's. Micro-narratives encourage dialogue and ultimately create debate. For Millennials/Zers, this is extremely important, if not fundamental: "Having a narrative and engaging in authentic experiences is a high priority in their personal lives, as well as in their careers."[6] There is no longer one explanation; each person possesses a valid opinion or, in more profound terms, a valid truth.

Millennials/Zers are willing to work hard but need to feel that their micro-narratives are being heard and understood. Effectively listening to Millennials/Zers is critical to understanding how to motivate them most effectively.[7] A student in my Executive MBA

*"*I don't understand your generation: why don't you just realize that you need to listen to us. We have great ideas and quicker ways of getting things done."
– Grant Diaz, supervisor (age 28)

class shared the story of a Canadian banking CEO who got on the elevator of his downtown Toronto office building with a new Millennial employee. The young employee wasted no time in introducing herself, saying, "I've been meaning to set an appointment with you to share my ideas. I'll give your secretary a call." Soon after, the elevator doors opened, and she disembarked and continued with her day. The CEO was stunned; the young employee, however, was unfazed. She had learned in her university classes that ideas have value, regardless of the age or experience of the person delivering them. This Millennial, like many others, had been taught to be confident and speak her mind since, according to her micro-narrative, this has value and the potential to change the CEO's business (and advance her career). So long as she remained polite and professional, she was correct to voice her thoughts.

Millennials/Zers consider themselves to be unique, more so than any previous generation. Each individual has their own story, informed by their own experiences and beliefs. In this sense, it is essential to consider the fact that each Millennial/Zer thinks somewhat differently; this is what leads to the unique micro-narratives. This can be attributed to the pervasiveness of access to the Internet and social media, which have profoundly shaped Postmodern values and made it possible for Millennials/Zers to share their personal opinion on every topic. Postmoderns feel that, because their opinions are out in the open, they matter; thus, they think that their experience and interpretation of the events in their lives must be correct. While in the past, works were published only by experienced authors, now Millennials/Zers have online platforms to voice their opinions freely. For example, it is not uncommon for Millennial/Zer "influencers" on Instagram to have over 250,000 active followers.[8]

Millennials/Zers typically absorb information at a faster rate than any Modern. The now-ubiquitous smartphones mean that many of them google many times a day; it is quite scary to see how often my students check their smartphones. They analyze situations with a combination of current knowledge and acquired information, as opposed to just career experience. Unlike their predecessors, Millennials/Zers "expect rapid retrieval of information, are adept at multitasking, predominantly use technology for social and professional communication, and require active involvement in learning."[9] "Despite many having been raised by helicopter parents and spending far more time in institutional settings, from daycares through college, Millennials are desperate to take off the bike helmets and engage with the world free of their elders' literal and metaphorical safety equipment."[10] Millennials/Zers are, to a considerable degree, the future of innovation, and therefore must be listened to.

Listen more, talk less is our first practical piece of advice. Despite misconceptions Moderns might hold, I firmly believe that Millennials are mature. They appreciate the time that is given to them by others and acknowledge that their ideas may be a little "out there." Nonetheless, they want Moderns to know that they are active thinkers who are looking for creative solutions to move your company forward. Moderns should not immediately discredit what they have not yet heard. What Moderns must understand and adapt to is that Millennials/Zers, who grew up in the digital age, require a different approach to communication than do Gen Xers or baby boomers.[11]

This approach is consistent with what the current business environment places immense value on in most organizations: innovation. New methods, new business models,

"Millennials are lovely people. They might challenge everything, including some things that we hold most dear, but they have incredible insight and bring a lot of energy. They are making our company richer by helping to drive innovation and we are better for it."
– Scott McDonald, global CEO, Oliver Wyman

"Millennials have a completely different mentality. They crave more freedom to express themselves and to produce an idea than prior generations."
– Fred Jalbout, CEO, Saco Technologies Inc.

and unique designs are all in increased demand and command a high premium. For example, in health care, the boomers will put greater demands on our systems, yet in the West, we can hardly afford to provide significantly more funding in health care. The solution? Better management of the health care resources already in use, and more innovation.[12] I am hard pressed to come up with an organization or industry that doesn't need more change.

While it is relatively easy to see that innovation is needed and desirable, it is more challenging to determine where innovation comes from. One of the best insights into innovation is that it often originates from the peripheral, outer limits of an organization. This is because the periphery possesses a higher degree of heterogeneity than the core of a company, which tends to be more homogenous. McGill University's Henry Mintzberg, an internationally renowned business management academic, argues that executives need to cut across the silos and slabs of a corporation to innovate effectively.[13] Mintzberg uses the term "silos" to refer to the functional areas of an organization, such as marketing, manufacturing, finance, and sales. He then uses "slabs" to refer to the hierarchical levels, typically front-line management, middle management, and the executive suite. He indicates that executives often fail to work with personnel of other standards (slabs) and in other disciplinary areas (silos). They simply adhere to the traditional model of sending their orders downward and following established corporate hierarchies. Innovation, however, is not limited to one group of people and certainly does not always originate at the top.[14] In an interview, Mintzberg used the example that "IKEA is in the business of selling unassembled furniture because a worker tried to put a table in his car and it didn't fit – so he took the legs off. Somebody was clever enough to say, 'Hey, wait a minute. If we have to take the legs off, [then] so do our customers.' That's how the most interesting strategy in the furniture business came to be – by a worker trying to put a table in a car."

Research has suggested that a homogeneous work environment most often leads to an organization being stuck in the past and becoming irrelevant.[15] Wayne Gretzky, the legendary former professional hockey player, was reputed to have said it best: "You don't go to where the puck is, you go to where it is going to be." If management truly desires innovation, heterogeneity in the workforce must be the ultimate goal.[16]

Even the way we use the physical workplace is evolving to become more innovation-friendly. Both the open-office concept and the idea of a personal desk are dying. Instead, we are witnessing the rise of flexible design, where different areas in the workplace are used to best fit the employee's task. One of my students went as far as to say they had no interest in ever having a personal office space in their career. Millennials/Zers value autonomy and the freedom to choose how to complete their work. While this discussion of innovation might seem to be a digression from the topic at hand – Millennials/Zers – the two are intrinsically related.

"[Tech] ceos have had to become much more thoughtful about culture, and they have to create workplaces where people actually want to go to work every day."
– Adam Bryant, columnist, Corner Office, *New York Times*

Culture of Innovation

Add diverse perspectives

Tap into the trenches of the organization

Share information across horizontal and vertical structures

Establish a flexible workplace

Value thinkers with fresh ideas who are newer to the industry

Figure 5.1
Steps toward building a culture of innovation

Millennials/Zers were practically born with the belief that heterogeneity and a diversity of perspectives lead to innovation. They honour diversity because it has, in their educational and extracurricular experiences, enabled them to grow, fine-tune their knowledge, shape their micro-narratives (and their truth), and, perhaps most importantly, be heard. Think of the incredible (and healthy) growth of equity, diversity, and inclusion (EDI) committees and initiatives in companies, universities, and governments. Universities across the world are teaching students to embrace group diversity and promoting diversity throughout their programs and curricula. Inspired by this movement at McGill, my university, I started a biweekly column in November 2020 called Indigenous Leaders, where an Indigenous medical doctor and I interview Indigenous leaders for the *Globe and Mail* newspaper.[17] Furthermore, and in contrast to the experience of generations past, diversity is a value embraced by society. Prejudice with regard to age, status, or level does not permeate the Millennials/Zers' worldview as it did for Moderns during the civil or women's rights movement. Millennials/Zers understand that they are in the trenches of an organization, and who better to consult than the person on the ground? Sometimes the bird's-eye view is not enough.

At the root of embracing diversity is a will to change corporate culture. As detailed in the *Handbook of Industrial and Organizational Psychology*: "Managing diversity means changing the culture – that is the standard operating procedure. It requires data, experimentation and the discovery of the procedures that work best for each group. It is more complex than conventional management but can result in more effective organizations."[18] Listening plays a huge role in managing diversity. However, for Millennials/Zers to be effectively involved in innovation and lend their diverse perspectives, more than listening is required. To Millennials/Zers, a senior-level manager reaching out to a young person for advice is a priceless experience and is the ultimate sign of real respect.

As we are already aware, young people have voices and strive to be heard. While their thoughts may not be as refined as their managers', their ideas are more likely to be innovative, given their diverse outlook and unique perceptions. Furthermore, because they learn quickly, these skills can be effectively targeted to address problems specific to your organization. In short, your fresh flock of young minds is ripe and malleable. Millennials/Zers may not yet fully understand your corporate culture or industry, but that is irrelevant. Increasingly, we hear the argument that people without industry experience are valuable to promoting innovation at a company because they bring new views that allow you to "think outside the box."[19]

This trend has been seen on a macro level in multiple industries where a non-experienced disruptor enters a field and, simply due to their unconventional way of doing things, dominates the industry. For example, Amazon in the book industry, LinkedIn in the recruitment industry, Uber in transport, Airbnb in accommodation, and Apple in personal computing have all, in relatively short order, overturned the existing dynamic of their respective industries. Thankfully, there is a place for some grey hairs. While innovation is important, Silicon Valley proves its mantra that you need a few adults in the mix to bring wisdom and experience. However, those adults must be willing to listen and learn.

Isabelle Hudon, at the time a senior executive at Sun Life Financial and now president and CEO of the Business Development Bank of Canada, pivoted her marketing career to an entirely new sector: insurance. In her first six months at Sun Life, Hudon spent hours meeting with employees in small groups of ten. Her experience in those first six months underscores the importance of senior members of an organization listening to and learning from their younger colleagues. As she recounts: "It's amazing what you can learn by asking the right questions and listening to your colleagues. My goal was to be able to take the elevator and make eye contact with my colleagues, and [that they wouldn't] look at the floor and say, 'Oh my goodness, that's the president.'"[20] Hudon wanted to listen to her new employees to foster trust and respect and facilitate an environment where openness and information sharing are valued. To engage Millennial/Gen Z employees and promote an optimal working environment, Moderns must simply listen.[21]

The need for developing and executing more effective strategies is another key reason why executives must listen more.[22] Long gone are the days of deliberate strategy development, an approach perhaps best characterized by Harvard's Michael Porter's models, including his famous "Five Forces and Three Generic Strategies," along with various acronyms such as PESTLE, SWOT, etc.[23] These ideas are still taught to MBAS and undergrads alike. They need to know them, as they are an essential part of the lexicon of strategy development.

"Leaders need to remember that they have two ears and one mouth; they should use them in that ratio. Listening is critical for successful leadership."
– Mairead Lavery, president and CEO, Export Development Canada

However, a different view, using Henry Mintzberg's idea of emergent strategy, appears to be on the rise, both in practice and in academic circles. Mintzberg's model views strategy as a set of actions (or behaviours) that are consistent over time: "A realized pattern [that] was not expressly intended" in the initial planning process.[24] Emergent strategy implies that an organization is learning what works (and what doesn't) in practice and continuously applying this in real time. If this is the world in which your organization operates (and I am hard pressed to think of an industry for which it is not), then the CEO and their C-suite team have no choice but to pay attention to a broader source of information, opinions, and approaches. There is no longer room for a this-is-how-it's-always-been-done mentality. Active listening, especially with Millennials/Zers who will form the future leadership, is the only way to develop a viable, well-informed strategy. The full picture is never fully disclosed through a single source. A comprehensive outlook is acquired by informal communication with as many sources as possible.

Yet for too many Moderns, and I must admit that this applies to me at times, "the purpose of listening is to seize the first available moment to reinforce your position, to counter the other person or to move on to the next subject. In other words, you're not really listening. It's all about you, it's all about your strategic desires [and] the next thing you want to do or say."[25] By contrast, the type of listening required to develop an optimal strategy "demands to be fully present and ready to respond to what might get thrown your way." All too often, however, especially for Moderns, "our listening shuts down when we're anticipating what might happen next."[26] In response, Sara Stibitz recommends getting over a need to talk or interject by adopting an attitude that will allow you to hear what's being shared.[27] This involves an appreciation and accommodation of the unique characteristics of the Millennial/Gen Z mind.

> "For me, it's trying to bring [Millennials] around the table. How do you create these occasions where you bring [in] the younger people? They're seeing [technology] from a different place – they've grown up with technology, we've learned to adapt to technology – so what does that change in our perspective?"
> – Nathalie Pilon, president, ABB Canada

Authors and company co-founders Amy Jen Su and Muriel Maignan Wilkins describe another significant barrier to listening by describing a manager who, in trying to be more assertive and in ensuring that she always offered her point of view in meetings, came off as having prematurely made up her mind.[28] To counter this problem, they advise managers to listen open-mindedly and be willing to have their opinions changed. They indicate that Moderns should "go in with the assumption that your colleagues and employees are smart too, and therefore might have a good reason for having a different position on an issue." Moderns need to appreciate and accept the value that Millennials/Zers bring to the workplace and – for the benefit of their own business and Millennials/Zers' satisfaction – demonstrate this to their employees by actively listening.

We now turn to several other strategies Moderns can use to become more effective listeners, and how Moderns can derive more value from the conversations they have with Millennials/Zers at work.

Strategies for
Effective Listening

The concept of listening is not new. However, the phenomenon of executives listening to young people in their organization is. A re-

" I favour listening. As a leader, I have learned to listen more than talk."[29]
– Dr Peter Goldberg, head of critical care, McGill University Health Complex

search project at the Stanford Graduate School of Business examined how boards of directors rate CEOs.[30] In this survey, directors rated CEOs high in decision-making abilities but low in people-management areas. The report specifically indicates a lack in the specific skills needed to manage Millennials, including listening: "In addition to 'mentoring' and 'developing talent,' 'listening' and 'conflict management' were the skills least mentioned as strengths for a CEO."[31] To effectively manage Millennials/Zers, "each of these should be at least in the top five of a CEO's strengths because they are critical components to excelling in the CEO role."[32]

The fact that these are the skills in which CEOs were most deficient is symptomatic of a broader problem: listening is often completely overlooked – both academically and in practice – as a much-needed leadership skill. It is said that listening barely makes this cut. And when they do listen, leaders too often use the act of listening as part of their way of exerting power, influencing the direction of a meeting, or taking command of the conversation.

Listening is not always done in the collaborative manner that is needed. Compounding this problem is the fact that we spend anywhere from one-third to one-half of our time listening, yet we retain very little of what we hear.[33]

Listening is an incredibly overlooked leadership tool: when done well and encouraged, it creates a safe environment to share ideas and collaborate.[34] Daniel Lamarre, CEO of Cirque du Soleil, describes listening as one of the most important skills he brings to his leadership.[35] A *Harvard Business Review* article detailed: "Listening might feel passive – it's much faster to move to a decision based on the information you already have. But you risk missing important considerations and sacrificing the opportunity to connect. It takes time to truly listen to someone, but it pays dividends in the long run."[36]

One of the most important leadership lessons I learned from my early days at IBM that I later had to discard was the assumption that all leaders were extroverts. Today, introverts are recognized as valuable members of leadership teams.[37] I have been doing research and interviewing CEOs of large multinationals about introverts in the C-suite. To my considerable surprise, between 25 per cent and 30 per cent of executives in the C-suite, according to my research, are introverts. Because it can be a Darwinian struggle to make it to this leadership level at large firms, these introverts must be very capable leaders. Perhaps unsurprisingly, to a fair degree it comes down to the topic of this chapter: *listening*.

Indeed, from the perspective of the CEOs that I have interviewed, one of the key strengths of introverts is that they tend to be much better listeners than extroverts. This is mainly because introverts, by their very nature, like to reflect and think before they comment. Extroverts, on the other hand, are often quite articulate (some are even eloquent), but they are often too quick to jump in and fill the silence with their words. What extroverts say might be well presented, but it is not always thoroughly thought out or reasoned. A key lesson from this research for me, an extrovert, is that I need to channel my inner introvert at times and become a better listener to be a better leader.

There are different types of listening, some more effective than others. Melissa Daimler, head of learning and organizational development at Twitter, argues that there are three levels of listening: internal listening, focused listening, and 360 listening.[38] These vary in the degree to which one can receive and respond to the information the sender is attempting to deliver. Internal listening entails focusing on your thoughts, worries, and priorities, even as you pretend to be focusing on the speaker. Focused listening involves being able to focus on the speaker but still not connecting fully with them to form a relationship. You may be nodding in agreement, but you might not be picking up on the nuances of what the other person is saying. The act of 360 listening means that there is a connection and an energy linking the speaker and the listener. You are listening to what the other person is saying, and also paying attention to how they are saying it, and what they are not saying.

To achieve 360 listening – as part of fully engaged, impactful, and energetic conversations – leaders can adopt two strategies put forth by Daimler. The first is eye contact; listeners are encouraged to put away their electronic devices in meetings, and, for the other end of the conversation, to encourage employees to do the same. In her thoughtful book, *Reclaiming Conversation*,[39] Sherry Turkle summarizes these strategies when she writes that "we face a significant choice. It is not about giving up our phones, but about using them with greater intention. Conversation is there for us to reclaim." Secondly, Daimler suggests creating space in your day to have meaningful conversations and to listen deeply to others. When she has back-to-back meetings, Daimler indicates that her goal is to schedule them with just enough time to run to the next meeting. However, when she strategically creates space in her agenda to reflect on a specific conversation and prepare for the next meeting, she feels that she can be more present for others and give them her full attention.[40]

Another name for the incorporation of these strategies in achieving what Daimler calls 360 listening might be empathic (or active) listening. I strongly recommend that executives practise this optimized type of listening as much as possible, especially when dealing with their Millennial employees, as this is something to which they will immediately respond. Since so much workplace communication happens using e-mail, managers must be mindful of ways to engage and interact with their Millennial/Gen Z workforce that incorporate more meaningful listening. I now turn to additional strategies to achieve this type of optimal, active listening.

Active Listening

Active listening is not a novel concept; indeed, a significant amount of research has been conducted on the topic.[41] Researcher Christine Riordan suggests that, based on empirical research, active listening, combined with empathy – attempting to understand a situation from another person's point of view – is the most effective form of listening.[42] In her work, she advances three key behaviours for more effective active listening. The first is to recognize the full range of verbal and non-verbal cues that might arise in a conversation, including verbal tone, facial expression, and other forms of body language. Body language, in this sense, is critical; there have been several excellent books written on the topic. One that I particularly like is *Winning Body Language* by Mark Bowden.[43] Most experts agree that we communicate much more through our body language than by the words that we use. In sum, during a conversation, leaders

"When I can sense that my superiors are listening to me and valuing my opinions despite my relative inexperience, I feel a stronger connection to my company. This kind of attention makes me feel more comfortable and willing to take risks and openly share ideas."
– Pamela Garnett, consultant, EY Toronto (age 24)

must learn to receive all of the information, verbal and non-verbal, that the sender is communicating. Ultimately, leaders must learn to truly listen, with all of their senses, not just through hearing. Great leaders (and listeners) also pay attention to what others are not saying and learn to probe. In this sense, excellent leaders must also understand how others are feeling and acknowledge those feelings, making those with whom they are conversing feel appreciated and heard.

Excellent leaders also understand how others are feeling and acknowledge those feelings. As discussed in chapter 3, emotions matter very much in the Millennials/Zers' worldview. Riordan suggests sample phrases that can be used to show you recognize the emotions of others. Some of them are: "Thank you for sharing how you feel about this situation, it is important to understand where everyone is coming from on the issue; would you like to share a bit more on your thoughts on this situation?; You seem excited (happy, upset, etc.) about this situation, and I would like to hear more about your perspective."[44]

Riordan further recommends a second active listening behaviour, referred to as processing, which encompasses what we generally associate with good listening.

Processing involves understanding the meaning of the messages and keeping track of the points of the conversation. An excellent active listener can summarize the points of agreement and disagreement that are brought forth during a conversation. By using these key conversational points, listeners can subtly indicate to the speaker that they are listening actively and that the speaker is being heard. Larry Bossidy, former CEO of Honeywell, was renowned for listening very effectively. His strategies are, therefore, instructive: he "divided a sheet of paper about three-quarters across. On the larger left side, he scribbled detailed notes; on the smaller right side, he occasionally jotted down two or three words, capturing what he perceived to be the key insights and issues being brought to his attention."[45]

Finally, Riordan's research suggests a third behaviour: active responding.[46] Effective use of this behaviour assures the speaker that they are being listened to and encourages active communication to continue further. Riordan details that leaders who are effective responders give appropriate replies through verbal acknowledgements, insightful clarifying questioning, and paraphrasing of what they've heard. They also use non-verbal cues, such as facial expressions, eye contact, and overall body language.

Other effective responses might include head nods and full engagement in the conversation with spoken acknowledgements, e.g., "that is a great point."[47]

Effective active listening is also crucial in terms of building rapport with a leader's subordinates and, ultimately, in developing those intangible qualities to which all leaders aspire: charisma and presence. In her excellent and practical book, *The Charisma Myth*, Olivia Fox Cabane discusses the overlap between charisma and listening. She usefully divides charisma into three elements: power, warmth, and presence. Appearing powerful means that others see us as being able to affect the world around us through influence, authority, wealth, expertise, intelligence, social status, or any combination thereof. Warmth, she suggests, is goodwill toward others. Communicating warmth tells others whether a leader is likely to use whatever power they have in favour of others – being perceived as warm means being perceived as having some of the following qualities: benevolence, altruism, and a willingness to make the world a better place.

However, of these qualities, the third, presence, is most relevant to the discussion at hand. Presence speaks to the degree to which one is engaged in a conversation and able to hold the attention of others. There is a definite problem among leaders today with being able to engage an audience in conversation, a situation that has only been worsened by the omnipresence of smartphones that too many of us sneak glances at while others are speaking. General Martin Dempsey has noticed nineteen-year-old privates texting while talking to him. One can scarcely imagine how the older generation would have responded to this: imagine General George Patton pulling out his silver-plated Colt pistol, shooting the offending party, then asking, "Does anyone else have something to text?"[48] Presence, in this sense, is intrinsically tied to active listening. Cabane argues that merely being present when listening is one of the most charismatic things a person can do. This idea is supported by one of the most charismatic leaders of our times, Bill Clinton. Many observers have commented that a key element of his charisma as a leader is that he is fully focused on making each individual in his audience feel as if they are the only other person in the room, mainly by incorporating many of the active listening strategies discussed above.[49]

When they do listen, senior executives tend to listen primarily to their direct reports. This approach works reasonably well in a stable and static world where everything operates as "business as usual." However, our world is in the midst of turbulent times and these rules no longer apply. In the VUCA (volatile, uncertain, complex, ambiguous) world, executives cannot limit the scope of their communications within an organization. Instead, they must reach out across the organization to obtain a more comprehensive view of the operations and achieve innovation. In our Postmodern age, the truth of the matter is that "truth" no longer resides exclusively at the top. Two essential books focus on the need for executives to spend more time listening: *Power Listening: Mastering the Most Critical Business Skill of All* by Bernard Ferrari[50] and *Talk Inc.* by Harvard Business School professor Boris Groysberg and former *Fast Company* managing editor Michael Slind.[51] Both books identify a significant correlation between strong decision-making capabilities and listening skills.

Executives must, therefore, realize that every individual in an organization has something valuable to contribute; after all, that is why they were hired and retained. As listeners, executives must not only listen but listen actively by being open, putting aside their own biases, and empathizing with others. An open mind is essential to be an effective leader in the Postmodern world. Millennials/Zers strongly believe that they should be heard and that their ideas are valuable and unique. They are the technological wizards of the digital age. They are some of the most ambitious people you will find. They have given your product or service much creative thought. Why not consult them and make them feel valued?

" I think what is clear is the Millennials are the best-educated generation ever."
– Frank Kollmar, president and CEO, L'Oreal Canada

So, whether their goal is to become more in touch with the times and with their Millennial/Gen Z workforce, or to drive better strategies and more innovation at their companies, Modern leaders should develop practical active listening skills.[52] Indeed, they will quickly learn that these two goals are not mutually exclusive: becoming more in touch with the Millennial workforce, as I have indicated, enables the development of more innovative strategies and, thus, very much helps drive innovation. What Millennials/Zers do know is how to think. Provide them with the missing pieces and let them wow you. They are eager to please, especially

What is it?

- Speaker and listener are linked by connection and energy
- Act of actively listening to what is said and how it is delivered

How to achieve it?

- Recognize full range of verbal and non-verbal (i.e., body language, tone) cues
- Understand and acknowledge emotions
- Process what is being said by keeping track of main points and summarizing
- Do not pre-empt potential answers
- Actively respond by returning appropriate verbal and non-verbal cues

Why?

- Builds rapport with subordinates, developing charisma and presence
- Improves decision-making capabilities and expands perspectives
- Enables the development of more innovative strategies

Figure 5.2
Brief summary of active listening

when they are consulted directly. All it takes is a little faith and the ability, and choice, to listen more and talk less.

This cannot be an act; Millennials/Zers must feel that they are truly being listened to. The act of listening must be authentic; being real is a driving force for Millennials/Zers. To be successful, these strategies must be (and appear to be) and genuine. The strategies for active listening noted above cannot be taken and mechanistically applied. Being an authentic leader to effectively lead Millennials/Zers is the subject of the next chapter.

6

The Importance of Authenticity
Self Lost, and Self Regained

Living as one's authentic self is a goal for many members of all five generations alive today – seniors, boomers, Gen X, Millennials, and Generation Z – but it perhaps figures most prominently for the latter two. Being authentic has meant something different for each generation – the concept has evolved. This chapter focuses on the meaning of the idea, and on what it means to provide authentic leadership to Millennials and Zers. It is critical to this group, so if you are, Millennials/Zers will appreciate you more than they do those who are not.

> **I** think one of the key things you need to think [about], as a leader, is transparency and being true to yourself. For me, the 'walk the talk' is critical."
> – Nathalie Pilon, president, ABB Canada

Leaders often struggle with being authentic. Donna Ladkin and Chellie Spiller's book, *Authentic Leadership: Clashes, Convergences and Coalescences*,[1] includes chapters cataloguing the leadership styles of great leaders such as Nelson Mandela, Mother Theresa, and George Washington, all of whom, the authors argue, struggled to remain their true selves. The thought of this should be of comfort to the Modern leader struggling with the same issue.

As previously mentioned, the Postmodern worldview is greatly influenced by information and communications technology (ICT), which enables rapid access to a plethora of information in a variety of formats, including social media platforms such as Facebook, Instagram, TikTok, WhatsApp, LinkedIn, and Twitter. The use of these by the Millennial/Z generations makes it considerably more difficult for leaders to simulate or "fake" their image. Any attempt to do this automatically broadcasts the "inauthentic" message and results in a loss of credibility. People – especially Millennials/Zers – can use the Internet to learn relatively quickly almost anything that is public knowledge about a person, and can put any stories they may have been told to the test. In the Millennial/Gen Z world, everyone has the means to be a fact-checker, with almost no effort.

It is amazing what people can know about you before they even meet you. Strangers can obtain a great deal of information about you by simply googling your name and perusing your Facebook page or LinkedIn profile. When I have a meeting scheduled in Outlook calendar, I receive a LinkedIn profile of the person I am meeting with. This obviates the first part of a conversation about a person, since I already have access to their professional profile – a profile that has been carefully crafted (usually) to present the individual in a way that puts their best foot forward. It might still be possible to maintain a lower profile online, but increasingly this takes a considerable amount of effort. Indeed, seeing someone with little or no online presence makes most Millennials/Zers skeptical, and may itself bring into question the authenticity or competency of that person. For Millennials/Zers, having a lower profile is far less important than the requisite balancing act between having a public image, and limiting access to online personal details to close friends and family. This strikes Xers as contrary to their experience, but the online world evolves quickly.[3]

> "There is so much information online about almost everyone nowadays, it is very difficult not to develop any sort of bias or preconceived notions about others prior to meeting them."
> – Michael Roche, business student, Fordham University (aged 25)

> "As a Millennial, I have several versions of 'true self.'[2] As a student leader I channelled my assertiveness and charisma, while as a consultant, I was channelling my ability to listen, apply myself, and learn. Being authentic means understanding that being 'myself' can present differently in different circumstances, but that I stay true to my core values, regardless of the role I play."
> – Lainie Yallen, consultant, BCG Toronto (age 24)

So, what exactly is authenticity? Though they often struggle to come up with a detailed definition of what genuine authenticity is, Millennials/Zers frequently mention several overarching concepts that encompass it. It appears that "being comfortable with oneself" and "knowing who one is" are the most relevant attributes of Postmodern authenticity.

From an academic perspective, authenticity, it seems, can be viewed from two perspectives: constructive and existential. Constructive authenticity refers to the cultural context (or constructs) of what is considered to be authentic. At the other end of the spectrum, existential authenticity refers to that which is necessitated by the current pressures of societal expectations, norms, and values.[4] Constructive authenticity is intrinsically tied to the cultural context in which authenticity is conceptualized. Social media has enabled Millennials/Zers to communicate their true feelings to a massive audience without the fear of being judged, at least personally. However, social media also allows them to represent and sometimes distort information to fulfill their agendas, without having to face significant consequences if they are caught doing so. In short, social media and networking sites provide an outlet for endless self-expression. With this freedom, however, conflict arises as Millennials/Zers attempt to reconcile how they present themselves online with their actual (offline) persona. They can post a "happy" status update with a smiley face to mask their true emotions; without knowing them intimately offline, few will be the wiser to their real situation.

In some cases, they might feel that the simple act of making a post, and the influx of reactions and comments that it will hopefully produce, will in and of itself make them happy. They can shape themselves to appear differently; they want their online peers to perceive them as adventurous, successful, fashionable, athletic – thereby fulfilling the social expectations of other users. They may even "present" differently to different online groups of people (some of which may be in opposition to each other) as a means of infiltrating the "other" side, or just because they can. In real life (IRL), however, it would be much more difficult to achieve this and maintain the ruse.

Millennials/Zers may go so far as to merge their offline and (some of) their online worlds, adopting elements of their online avatar(s) in the real world, thereby modifying their authentic self. This changing nature can make the "true self" hard to pin down for any length of time. In the age of social media, authenticity for Millennials/Zers is characterized by the consistency and continuity between their online personas and their lives. The more congruence there is between the two, the more authentic a person will appear to be to their peers.

However, authenticity may also be defined existentially, that is to say, by overarching social norms, values, and expectations.[5] Why is it important to consider authenticity from this perspective? Because Millennials/Zers want to be able to be themselves and thus reject this existential conception of authenticity in favour of the constructive definition. Millennials/Zers are not interested in playing "the game" – adapting their personalities to societal norms and expectations – as their boomer parents once did. Indeed, for many boomers, the cost of playing the game was too high: failed marriages, too much travel, too little work-life balance, and loss of meaningful contact with their children cost them dearly. And all of this, sadly, only to often end up being fired by their employer later in life, in some cases without a pension after years of loyalty. Reacting to the pressures that many of their parents felt, Millennials/Zers refuse to adapt and conform to the same corporate personae their parents once epitomized. Too often their parents got fired by "the Man," which has led them to distrust corporations that offered life-long employment but reneged on the promise. They want their employers to respect their differences (their micro-narratives, as discussed in the previous chapter) and embrace the potential that these unique qualities can bring. Corporations, however, expect workers – Postmodern or Modern – to conform to their existing corporate culture, even as it is in the process of being updated for the new millennium.[6] From the 1950s onward,

"Every employee is different. A good CEO needs to be attentive to that."
– Catherine Dagenais, president and CEO, SAQ

there has been a rise in the concept of the "organization man";[7] workers are expected not only to be qualified for the job itself but also to be a good fit for the specific business unit in which they will work, and with the existing culture of the organization. In an attempt to conform to these restrictive and possibly outdated expectations, Millennials/Zers are forced to hide their true feelings and engage in emotional acting, another example of emotional labour. They project the feelings that they feel are "appropriate" for the situation at hand. The very expectation that they obey the rigid rules and guidelines of the company – especially concerning corporate culture, but also for something as simple as a dress code – runs counter to the Postmodern worldview, which values individualism and diversity. This restricts Millennials/Zers' ability to show who they truly are.[8]

Within this context, we should not forget that Millennials/Zers tend to be idealistic. They have vast stores of energy and, perhaps in stark contrast to their Modern counterparts, hope. They want to believe that every person's

❜❜ | am most valuable to an organization when I am fully able to express myself, from my ideas to my appearance. I am not interested in the rigidness of rules, which stifle creativity or individuality."
– Samah Syed, human kinetics student, University of Ottawa (age 26)

apparent character represents who they truly are; this is called the authentic self. In this sense, they believe that the culture within organizations will encourage and enable this authenticity.

Nonetheless, the reality of the environment in which Millennials/Zers find themselves is not as rosy as they may have anticipated. This may account for a high degree of workplace dissatisfaction and low retention rate among Millennial/ Gen Z workers. However, this should not lead us to believe that a corporate culture that supports the expression of the authentic self is a utopian pipe dream. Given the current issues with workplace authenticity, it should be acknowledged that certain obstacles are put in place by Moderns that must be understood and removed for the workplace to become an environment that promotes Millennials/Zers' authentic self to become a reality.

Socrates once said, "No one knowingly does evil," yet we may well ask why so many unethical actions occur in our society today. Building upon the powerful assumption that all humans are born inherently good, Han Wang – a Postmodern and recent former student of mine now working in LA – acting as the resident philosopher for this chapter, highlights in the next section a few of the behavioural biases that he feels he is most susceptible to. He then goes on to explain just how to assist Postmoderns in regaining their sense of self.

Self Lost

Millennials/Zers constantly feel that they have a vast sea of ambition to conquer. Though they may not have a clear idea of where they'll be in ten years, they know that they want it to be someplace grand. After all, this is the generation that was always told that they could change the world, and they believed it. In this sense, they are perhaps the epitome of Renaissance thought: that is, they each believe that they are at the centre of the universe. This presents a source of great inspiration and danger for Millennials/Zers; while it fuels their ambition, they can also be consumed by self-involvement and succumb to vices such as selfishness.

Millennials/Zers' sense of self, their goals, and their values are constantly shifting. Although everyone would like to think they are people of absolute integrity, everybody has a price for which they are willing to betray their morals. The following anecdote illustrates this idea.

A criminal comes to the office of a well-respected lawyer in town and, after admitting guilt for his crimes, asks the lawyer to defend him. The lawyer, with a deep sense of integrity and justice, refuses. The criminal offers to pay more. The lawyer again refuses. The criminal continues to offer more money. The lawyer becomes agitated and unceremoniously ejects the criminal from his office. The criminal then asks, "Why did you throw me out now, and not at the first or second offer?" The lawyer replies, "Because you were nearing my price!" That lawyer was Abraham Lincoln.

For Millennials/Zers, this crisis of conscience is even more profound and dynamic. The integrity with which Millennials/Zers go about their daily work can be viewed as a case of the classic law of supply and demand. Millennials/Zers' response to organizational hierarchies and organizational culture (demand) will vary depending upon how compatible those are with their values and desires (supply).

Millennials/Zers' responses to authority and hierarchy are incredibly variable, depending on the particular circumstances they find themselves in. Although organizational hierarchy is not as prevalent as it was twenty or thirty years ago, studies have shown that there is an innate quality of the human psyche that respects and, at times, blindly and carelessly obeys authority figures.

Perhaps the most notable example of authority and obedience is the set of experiments conducted by Stanley Milgram of Yale University in the early 1960s.[9] Participants were told that the experiment's purpose was to examine the effect of punishment on memory. They were instructed to give increasingly more significant electric shocks – which were indicated to participants as being real but were in actual fact only simulated – to "subjects": confederates hidden from view, but who they could speak with via intercom. For each wrong answer, the participant increased the strength of the "shocks" by 15 volts, up to a maximum of 450 volts (at which point a single shock would be fatal). The experiment, in actuality, was designed to evaluate the participants' compliance to commands that they believed were harmful to the subject. When prompted by expressions of authoritative language, would they continue to deliver the shocks at fatal levels? Despite the screams, pleadings, and eventual silence (simulating loss of consciousness or death), participants continued to obey the instructions of the authority figure and administered increasingly powerful shocks. They continued to administer the shocks despite their belief that they were potentially killing another person because they were told that they would not be held responsible for the outcome. With all responsibility for the consequences of their actions assumed by the authority figure, they felt able to relax their moral aversion to harming others.

While Millennials/Zers would generally like to believe that they would not obey the authority figure, the evidence is clear – two-thirds of participants followed the instructions. Variations of the Milgram experiments have been replicated several times since his original work; sadly, it appears that, under the right circumstances and given the right stimuli, almost anyone's moral values can be shifted.[10]

Self Regained

Authenticity is an essential and undeniable quality, that is, to stay true to one's values. The pursuit of authenticity is an ongoing process (hence the use of the word "pursuit"). It should be thought of as a project of self-creation, shaped by three crucial factors: *enlargement, connection,* and *aspiration,* which parallel the three aspects of one's past, one's relationships, and one's future (see figure 6.1). In reflecting upon our past experiences, we can enlarge our perspective. In broadening our perspective, we can better understand our relationships with others. Finally, in understanding the relationships we hold, we can remake and continue to pursue our aspirations.

However, in addition to this self-centred approach to authenticity, we must also recognize the relational aspect of the authentic self to the wider community. Our human, empathic nature allows that our aspirations are not limited

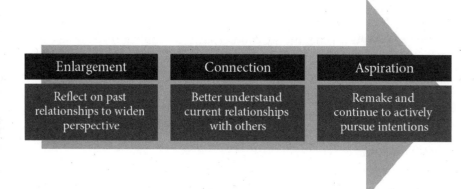

Figure 6.1
Pursuit of authenticity through a self-awareness and self-creation process

to individual needs but are also inclusive of the social concerns of the community. The simultaneous aspiration of connecting the self with the community shows that the pursuit of authenticity cannot be only a self-centric endeavour. It is an inherently relational project. Therefore, in the management context, rather than thinking about personal aspirations being selfish, we should look to integrate the aspirations of the employee and of the organization. This does not need to be something as commonplace as a correlation between salaries/bonuses and profits but, more profoundly, can involve an employee's fulfilment and a company's desire for innovation or diversity. Moderns, as the majority leaders, can create such relationships by embracing Millennial/Gen Z values and redefining the corporate culture in a more positive light. Examples of this might include environmentally sustainable practices and the broad adoption of ethical business codes; the acceptance of minority groups promotes healthy diversity. An open-door, supportive community approach creates optimal conditions for authentic self-pursuit.

Moderns and Millennials/Zers must form a joint mentorship to hold each other accountable and remind each other of their respective values. Each generation has its strengths and limitations; it is, therefore, absolutely crucial for individu-

" **M**oney is not enough to make workers satisfied. It makes it easier to swallow.*"*
– Associate, Stikeman Elliott LLP

als from all generations to work together to achieve common goals and aspirations. Effective mentorship is a two-way process in which we both teach
and learn from our generational counterparts. Having a professional confi-
dante to talk to – whether Modern or Millennial/Gen Z – is an extremely valuable asset that can help us realize where we stand in the pursuit of our
authentic self. It is up to Moderns, as leaders, to promote authenticity both
through their authentic leadership and by building a workplace that fosters
authenticity between Millennial/Gen Z and Modern employees.

What Is Authentic Leadership?

Many leaders fail to appreciate the fullness of the authentic leadership concept.
It speaks to the multiple-personality situation, where one is a different person
at work and outside of work; in a sense, the person has two distinct identities.
But which is the true identity?

When it comes to their leaders, Millennials/Zers want to uncover their true
identity and get to know the real person. They want someone who demonstrates a similar level of intensity and passion to theirs, but they do not want
this passion to be inauthentic or simulated. Mitch Kosh, senior vice president
of global human resources at Ralph Lauren Corporation, indicates the practical attributes that make up authentic leadership: "Millennials/Zers look for
adults who are as alive and as passionate, and as on fire and energetic, and
can really tell a story with a sense of wisdom and inclusion."[11]

Research has suggested that, in order to promote this type of authentic
leadership at the group level, there must be a shared culture of four qualities:
confidence, optimism, hope, and resilience.[12] Authentic leadership, when
properly utilized throughout an organization, leads to a positive relationship
with employees and results in increased hope, creativity, job satisfaction, and
team commitment.

An important implication of authentic leadership in this sense is that, despite Millennials/Zers' individualistic nature, their performance is affected by
the leadership of Moderns. Just as important as Millennials/Zers' pursuit of
their authentic self, Moderns must similarly pursue their authenticity and ex-
hibit similar values to Millennials/Zers to demonstrate authentic leadership.
In effect, they must lead by example. Managers and executives must admit to

their vulnerabilities and own up to their mistakes in seeking out their authenticity,[13] since "the effort to suppress who we are, takes away from what we do."[14] Finally, Millennials/Zers look for transparent, ethical leaders whom they can emulate.[15] Authentic leadership also becomes essential in this context, as it appears that part of being an open leader is increasingly becoming about more openness around the salaries, perks, and privileges enjoyed by leaders.[16]

Finally, it is important to ask: what does authentic leadership look like? Researchers describe a diverse array of elements; however, four appear consistently and prominently throughout the literature. Authentic leaders:

> "Millennials are value and purpose driven. They want transparency from leaders to ensure that they are contributing to an organization that is advancing their values."
> – Frank Kollmar, president and CEO, L'Oreal Canada

- are self-aware and genuine;
- are mission-driven and results-focused;
- lead with both heart and mind;
- focus on the long term.

Authentic leaders need to be *self-aware*, and *genuine* in their expression of who they are.[17] Before Moderns can encourage and support self-authenticity among Millennials/Zers, they must know their own strengths, limitations, and emotions. Cultivating this self-knowledge is being taught in leadership programs at some of the world's leading business schools. Being genuine means Moderns need to be willing to demonstrate not just their strengths but also their weaknesses and to be more open in communicating their feelings. These are critical factors to which Millennials/Zers are particularly responsive. In short, Moderns need to acknowledge their imperfections and mistakes openly.

Authentic leaders need to be *mission-driven* and *focused on results*. The focus is on their organization's mission and goals, not self-interest. They should not allow the lure of power, money, or ego to limit their ability to get the job done.[18] They must connect with people and motivate them to pursue common objectives. Authentic leaders embrace the idea of a community that is focused on doing something worthwhile in the world in a way that reflects excellence.

Authentic leaders *lead with their hearts, not just their minds*.[19] They are concerned with the well-being of the group as a whole. They follow a guiding set of empowering principles, which leads them to consider all actions that must be taken, insofar as the outcomes achieved result in increased well-being for the entire group. They adopt the basis of the Hippocratic Oath, which is often summarized today as "do no harm," in their everyday decisions and the ethos of the organization. They emphasize trust and respect to create an empathetic, supportive environment.

Authentic leaders *focus on the long term*.[20] They evaluate day-to-day activities and decisions throughout the organization in the context of possible future impacts. They strive for sustainable and enduring results, rather than those that are immediate and short-lived.

7

A Sense of Purpose
Work Must *Have Meaning*

It may be surprising, albeit comforting, to learn that at times, Moderns and Millennials/Zers can be remarkably similar. As boomers approach their sixties and seventies, they realize that a new life, after retirement, awaits them. They jump at the opportunity to reinvent themselves, working toward new goals and redefining their measures of self-worth. Millennials/Zers, interestingly, express these same aspirations at the beginning of their careers. Despite being many years away from retirement, they consistently question where they are going next, and many are asking themselves what gives their lives meaning, both within and outside the workplace. Perhaps most importantly, similar to their Modern counterparts, bringing value to the workplace and the world is essential to Millennials/Zers.[1] In *The Human Capital Edge*,[2] authors Bruce Pfau and Ira Kay found that across dimensions of generations, race, or gender, employees have generally always wanted the same things from work. To enjoy the work they do and the people with whom they work.[3] To derive a sense of purpose, a sense of meaning from work – that desire resonates with people of all ages. This chapter focuses on finding meaning and purpose at work – a fundamental need for

"What I heard at the Burger King information session is, 'Help us achieve our dream to be the #1 fast food service company in the world,' but all I can think is: Do I really want a career entirely devoted to worsening today's health epidemic? Is that the best dream I have for this world?"
– Steph Ambrose, BCom student, McGill University

"A brand name is no longer enough to attract top Millennial talent."
– Associate, Stikeman Elliott LLP

Millennials/Zers, and a concept that resonates with Moderns and other generations as well.

In the 1980s and early 1990s, workers' (Moderns') motivations seemed to
be much more financial in nature than they are today. The white-collar workers of the business world were very motivated by share prices; they did virtually everything they could to send company valuations higher. Thinking back
to my time working at IBM, I am hard pressed to remember why this was so
motivating. How things have changed!

While money is important to Millennials/Zers, and they do enjoy making
(and spending) it, it is not their primary focus, nor the reason why they go
to work every day. As with previous generations, Millennials/Zers long to find
purpose and be a part of something bigger than themselves. Perhaps the difference today is that information on the world, its problems and potential solutions, is so much more readily available than it was back then. A *Harvard
Business Review* article indicates that while "conventional wisdom holds that
Millennials/Zs are entitled, easily distracted, impatient, self-absorbed, lazy,
and unlikely to stay in any job for long," they are, more than anything, "looking
for purpose, feedback, and personal life balance in their work."[4] Meeting these
needs, and giving your young employees a sense of purpose, will allow them
to envision a future with your company. Young people are fickle: they are on
an endless search for happiness, but they want it all, and they want it instantaneously.
If an organization is unable to map out a ca-
reer road map and adequately define the purpose of employment for a Postmodern
employee, its management will experience a
high turnover among such employees in the
first two years of their employment. In-house
ping-pong tables and weekly wine-and-
cheese receptions are pleasant perks, but to
appeal to the stars of tomorrow, their work
must matter to them. For this reason, top em-

// | think there's more of a pre-
mium [for] today's Millennials on meaning. They long for –
which I think is a great strength –
meaningful work. They want to
be in a workplace where their
talents are appreciated and they
feel engaged in something that
matters."
– Amy Edmondson, Novartis
Professor of Leadership and
Management, HBS

ployers in the twenty-first century promise Millennials/Zers career coaching,
access to top business schools, and ongoing feedback so that Millennials/Zers
feel their careers have meaning and trajectory.

Some observers have said that Millennials/Zers are selfish – why would they behave any differently in the workplace? The fact is that they do not. Millennials/Zers view the workplace as a means to an end; it doesn't define them to the degree that it defined the entire life of many Moderns. Rather, Millennials/Zers want to lead an integrated life; while they want to be happy and excel on the job, above a certain minimum threshold, money is somewhat secondary. A recent study by Net Impact showed that the Millennial/Zers generation expects to make a difference in the world through their work, and thus find some kind of purpose. The same study shows that more than half of Millennials/Zers would take a 15 per cent pay cut to work for an organization that matches their values.[5]

"They want to work on meaningful things, and they also care that their company is a good company. And not just a good corporate citizen, but beyond that, that it takes good care of people – their own people, their customers – and that they put the right emphasis on the environment and on integrity. And so I think that's a very good thing as this younger generation comes into the business world, that it's making it not just okay but mandatory to care about those things and make sure that your company is reflecting those values."

– Angela Brown, CEO, Moneris

Of course, Millennials/Zers aren't the only ones who are serious about finding purpose in their work. Other generations would like to find it as well; after all, many of them are voicing the same concerns as their younger counterparts. A multi-generational study conducted by IBM back in 2015 found that approximately the same percentage of Millennials, Xers, and baby boomers want to make a positive impact on their organizations (21–25 per cent), help solve social and/or environmental challenges (20–24 per cent), do work that they are passionate about (20–23 per cent) – all with a high degree of work-life integration (18–22 per cent).[6] Unique to Millennials/Zers, however, is that they were found to be seeking purpose and meaning at such an early stage in their careers. This is part of a larger trend that has been observed in other studies. When asked about what their primary concern was during their first job, approximately 64 per cent of older Americans talked about making as much money as possible and learning new skills.[7] Fast-forward two decades, and it is apparent that Millennials/Zers are more motivated by issues other than money, some of which are outside of work. When asked the same question, younger Americans were much more likely to say that their top priority was

"Millennials/Zers, from my perspective, have a real passion for a variety of issues around community, fairness equality, diversity, lifestyle flexibility. And maybe more than the previous generations, they're willing to put their money where their mouths are: to leave companies that don't live up to their expectations as well as put a lot of pressure on companies to do those things."
– Scott McDonald, president and CEO, Oliver Wyman

doing something that they found enjoyable,[8] and that made a difference in society.[9]

Add to this the fact that Millennials/Zers are incredibly self-assured about their career potential, their confidence only being swayed in cases where their employer fails to provide them with a compelling vision for their future with the company. Imagine an airplane halted on the tarmac. The passengers are seated on board, the baggage is carefully stowed below, and the engines are revving. The pilot is waiting for the signal to go. This is precisely how Millennials/Zers feel if they are not provided with a clear sense of their future in a given role. They arrive with a hazy vision of the future but a clear desire to move forward. The pilot cannot leave without the approval of the air traffic controller: the message that clarifies things as being cleared for takeoff.

Similarly, Millennials/Zers cannot begin to commit their time and effort to a role without a clear sense of their future direction, and cannot grow without the guidance of their superiors. If their plane remains grounded without any clear indication of its eventual destination, they will disembark, return to the hangar, and embark on another plane. Millennials/Zers are ambitious and expect their employer to identify a clear-cut path toward future growth. Promotions, whether they include more compensation or not, are perceived as growth within the organization. When a future pathway is non-existent or too entangled with obstacles, working at that company becomes less alluring. If Millennials/Zers feel underutilized in their role and believe they're not being groomed as leaders, they may walk away from a role entirely.[10]

"You have to motivate [people], they have to see that you have a vision, and that's the important part. People will follow you if they see that they have a future with you."
– Laurent Beaudoin, CEO and chairman of the board, Bombardier

One possible explanation for this phenomenon is the neglect of Millennials/Zers' real needs by employers. Regardless of gender or geography, less than a third of Millennials/Zers feel that their current organizations are making full use of the skills they currently have to offer.[11] Most Millennials/Zers don't care about the bells and whistles found in many workplaces today – fancy latte machines, free food, and nap rooms.[12] Instead, purpose and career development drive this generation. As we have seen before, Millennials/Zers place the goal of finding a higher purpose through their work ahead of income; this might include opportunities to learn or grow, mentorship by high-quality managers, interest in the type of work they are doing, and opportunities for advancement.[13] Illustrating this, approximately 45 per cent of university graduates expect to obtain a leadership position within three to five years after graduation.[14] When organizations position themselves as growth platforms where people can develop faster than at the competition, retention becomes a non-issue.[15] Importantly, at the core of this explanation lies purpose; we will see that this is a common trend.

However, perhaps a better explanation may be sociological, based on the concept of loyalty. This explanation might broadly explain why, for Millennials/Zers, walking away from a job is significantly easier than it once was for their Modern counterparts. Many of today's workers, not solely Millennials/ Zers, no longer feel loyalty and commitment to their organization. In large part, this can be attributed to the volatility in the need for labour at many companies, not to mention the pain Millennials/Zers and their families experienced during the economic downturn of 2008 and its large-scale layoffs.[17] During that recession, Millennials/Zers witnessed their parents being laid off, without hesitation, by organizations to which they had been loyal and had dedicated years of their lives. Millennials/Zers understandably ask themselves, "Why be loyal to an organization that doesn't return that loyalty when the chips are down?" As a result, Millennials/Zers are loyal to roles or identities rather than to specific companies or organizations.[18]

A fairly recent survey conducted by Deloitte confirms this Millennial mindset with startling clarity. The study collected the views of nearly 7,700 Millennials in twenty-nine countries, all of whom had obtained a post-secondary

> "The sense of loyalty to one company has diminished significantly. Millennials are easily attracted to other firms outside of the company that they're working in, either because of impatience or because they want to progress more rapidly."[16]
> – Geoff Molson, owner, president and CEO, Montreal Canadiens nhl team, Bell Centre, and Evenko

> "Our generation is not as patient as prior generations."
> – Edgar Brown, BCom graduate, McGill University (age 23)

" It's not [that Millennials/Zers are] not loyal to a company, but [that] they're loyal to themselves first. And I think that's a really positive trait, where they're really pushing themselves and not becoming stuck in a dead-end job where they're not actually finding a way to revitalize themselves."
– Mark Hantho, global chairman of investment banking, Deutsche Bank

degree and were employed in large (100-plus employees) private-sector organizations.[19] The survey found that during the following year, if given the opportunity, 25 per cent of Millennials would quit their job to join a new organization or do something entirely different.[20] Asked about where they saw their career four years after the survey was taken, two out of three said they hoped to have moved on to new organizations.[21] Even Millennials in senior positions express the intention to leave their organizations relatively quickly.[22] Overall, 60 per cent of Millennials said that they were open to a different job opportunity, 15 percentage points higher than the percentage for non-Millennial workers.[23] This remarkable lack of loyalty presents a real challenge to any business currently employing a large number of Millennials, which, soon enough, will be almost every business.[24] Perhaps unsurprisingly in light of the above discussion, Millennials' degree of loyalty – that is, their decision to stay with or leave a company – strongly depends upon their ability to find meaning and purpose within their role.[25] This underscores the importance of giving Millennial employees a sense of purpose at work.

Indeed, while it has been well documented for the past two decades that employees under thirty-five years of age are more likely to move on to new opportunities, what has changed is the underlying reason for this: departing from the Modern pursuit of money, Millennials/Zers strive toward finding a greater sense of purpose. Deloitte's Millennial Survey found that while compensation might remain a powerful driver of employer choice, it certainly is not the only one. When Millennials/Zers are choosing between several organizations offering similar financial incentives, other factors come into play. When salary and other financial benefits are removed from the equation, work-life integration and opportunities to progress or take on leadership roles stand out as key motivators.[26] When Adam Poswolsky interviewed dozens of Millennials about their career choices for his book, *The Quarter-Life Breakthrough*, not once did any of his Millennial respondents indicate that they wanted to make lots of money, have lots of power, or retire with a pension in forty years.[27] Krista Alexander, KPMG's director of talent attraction, has commented that Millennials/Zers "are looking for meaningful work, and … for somewhere they can have an impact on the greater world and others. This generation wants to be challenged with important work that has meaning."[28]

Taking this constant search for meaning and purpose into account, it is unsurprising that Millennials/Zers are expected to hold fifteen to twenty positions throughout their working lives, many more than most Moderns could even imagine.[29] Nathaniel Koloc, co-founder and CEO of ReWork, a recruiting firm that places purpose-seeking professionals in social-impact jobs, illustrates this when he says, "There is no clear way 'up' anymore, it's just a series of projects or jobs, one after another. You can move in any direction; the only question is how you're devising your strategy of when to move and where you can 'land,' i.e., what you're competing for."[30] Effectively, Millennials/Zers determine their purpose and their career progress as simply a reflection of this. Millennials/Zers will inevitably shift and change careers as often as their self-concept changes.

> "When you work for the same company for thirty-seven years, it is very rare that the company will keep you on your toes or give you the challenges that you need to keep on growing. Some do, but most don't. I think the Millennials are right – when it starts feeling comfortable, fire yourself and go get another job."[31]
> – Patrick Pichette, former CFO, Google

This concept is perhaps best illustrated through the unique and inspiring career path of John Wood, founder of Room to Read, a global non-profit organization that promotes literacy and gender equality in education.[32] Prior to starting Room to Read, John held a senior position at Microsoft but left this life behind to deliver books on the backs of yaks to people in rural Himalayan villages. He detailed that "it wasn't an easy transition. I learned a lot at Microsoft, and I enjoyed it, but there was something inside me that felt that too many kids in the world today lose the lottery of life. I wanted to do something about it."[33] Like most Millennials/Zers' shifting sense of purpose, John's sense of personal purpose evolved. He left his corner office at Microsoft to pursue a better alignment between his sense of purpose and that derived from his work.

Careers like those at Room to Read appeal very much to many Millennials/Zers. The work gives them the sense that they are making a real difference regarding some of the genuinely important issues they feel the world is facing. Each year I speak to several hundred students and alumni about their careers.[34]

What has struck me over my extensive career in teaching is how the conversations have evolved over that time. Many more of the undergraduates and MBAS today are considering working for NGOS,[35] or at least for corporations that have serious, well-managed corporate social responsibility (CSR) programs. A particularly appealing option for many students is to work in those corporations' CSR programs, which, in theory, combines the meaningfulness of an impactful job with the financial security of a large firm. Search for meaning and purpose is on the agendas of most Millennials/Zers, not just in the Western world but increasingly in the developing economies as well. Without the ability to derive meaning and purpose from what they do, Millennials/Zers are unlikely to accept a position or to perform well in that position. Granted, not all Millennials/Zers feel this way; there will always be those who are willing to work extraordinary hours to make the "big bucks" and grasp the brass ring. However, these are now definitely fewer in number. Unless you are a world-renowned firm such as Google, McKinsey & Company, or Goldman Sachs, they aren't as apt to be interested in coming to work for you.

In direct response to this, a novel concept of leadership being put forward by McKinsey & Company, the World Economic Forum, and others is the need for tri-sector leaders to successfully tackle the world's most pressing issues. "Tri-sector leadership" is a term coined by Harvard professor Joseph Nye, defined as those able to engage and collaborate across the business, government, and social sectors.[36] Most often, these leaders have worked in at least two of the three industries and therefore have an in-depth and visceral understanding of their driving agendas and ways of doing things. It is beneficial if they have at least been exposed to the third sector, for example, by serving on an NGO or corporate board or on a government commission. In this sense, tri-sector leaders can engage Millennials/Zers on all levels, including their search for a purpose in the workplace. Ultimately, Millennials/Zers themselves will become tri-sector leaders due to their unique combination of skills, motivations, and perspectives.

Millennials/Zers want to feel in control of their careers. They experience a greater sense of control working in organizations that support their ambitions, align with their values, and feature a collaborative and trust-based culture: in short, factors that enable Millennials/Zers to have a strong sense of purpose. Those who feel in control appear to be more loyal and engaged. Unfortunately, a Gallup study conducted in 2016 found that only 26 per cent of Millennials are engaged, meaning that they are emotionally and behaviourally discon-nected from their job and company.[37] Not engaging workers sufficiently is a huge miss for organizations. Although, as noted previously, Millennials/Zers are often characterized as entitled job-hoppers, the reality is that most of this group is just not engaged at work. If a company is not able to engage Millen-nials/Zers and assist them in finding purpose, it seems improbable that Mil-lennials/Zers will stay loyal to that company.

Employee engagement tools that encourage work-life integration and em-ployee engagement in the workplace are designed to respond to these de-mands. Millennials/Zers want more than just an income.[38] They value happiness and do not necessarily equate wealth to happiness. As Jane Nayagam, vice-president of human resources at American Express Canada, eloquently puts it, "I believe the new generation of workers seek and entire package – training opportunities, global exposure and flexible work options. It is no longer just the amount on your paycheque."[39]

Furthermore, businesses must under-stand that, in this respect, the expectations of Millennials/Zers are vastly different from those of their Modern parents. As such, em-ployee engagement tools must accommo-date Millennials/Zers' unique needs; they cannot be designed based on the needs of their Modern predecessors. Merely giving a Millennial a raise may not be an effective strategy in this sense. As far as they are con-cerned, they want their employers to em-brace change and adapt to their needs, including, above all, their need to find a purpose in the work that they do. Busi-nesses must respond and adapt to this need. After all, Millennials/Zers are the future of all companies. How companies can react and adapt is the topic of the next section.

"[Millennials are] looking to learn, they're look-ing to advance, they're looking to do some interesting work. They're looking for stuff that has meaning and has some value. And if you don't give them an opportunity to contribute, and quickly, then they'll disengage."
– Sam Watts, CEO, Welcome Hall Mission/Mission Bon Accueil

"I truly want the company I work for to emulate my val-ues and principles. I feel that if my job directly contributes to bettering our society in some way, or making people's lives a little easier, I can be passionate about my role at the company."
– J.R. Venchrutti, associate, CIBC (age 25)

Creating Purposeful Organizations and Aligning Personal and Professional Purpose

Over the past several years, developing a meaningful sense of purpose has become a real strategic imperative for management executives. As Millennials/ Zers continue to make up an increasing part of our workforce, assisting and facilitating employees in finding a sense of purpose will only become a more essential role of leaders and managers. Organizations must focus more time and resources on developing meaning in the work they do and in having an organizational purpose, which gives people a genuine feeling that they are making the world a better place. I work with the Montreal Children's Hospital, where having a sense of meaning and purpose is almost a given for the nurses, doctors, and staff. The challenge is for global companies such as cosmetics firm L'Oréal and global banking giant Deutsche Bank to create an organization and corporate culture that Millennials/Zers can buy into as giving them a higher purpose in the work they do. To recruit and retain Millennial workers, organizations should promote a collaborative, team-based work environment (belonging) along with challenging and meaningful work (ego-status) instead of predictable salary, insurance, retirement, or other benefits (safety).[40] As Patrik Frisk, CEO of ALDO Group, expressed to me: "If you're able to clearly articulate to a Millennial why you're doing something and you can get them to buy in, they're completely on board; but if you fail to do that, then they turn off."[41] I fervently believe it can be done. Indeed, many companies have made very considerable progress in the past decade in this regard. So should yours.

Underscoring this is an understanding of what it means to have a purpose and how purpose can be defined. In his book, *The Purpose Effect*, Dan Pontefract explores the tripartite relationship between an individual's sense of purpose in life, an organization's purpose, and a person's purpose in their role at work. A personal sense of purpose is what motivates someone in their day-to-day life. By clearly defining its principles, ethics, leadership, and culture, an organization communicates its purpose to the world. Finally, the reason why a particular role exists in an organization is role purpose.[42] When all three of these aspects of purpose are adequately defined and well-aligned, the employee, organization, and society all benefit.[43] Pontefract uses the term *sweet spot* for this balanced state.[44] Any lack of alignment among the three categories of purpose can have devastating consequences at both an individual and a collective level.[45] It is up to employers to ensure that this balance is viable for their employees.

Personal purpose is the endless journey to develop, define, and decide the what, who, and how of one's life. One must ask questions such as: What am I doing to evolve myself? Who am I in life and at work? How will I operate and be perceived by others?[46] Millennials/Zers reflect on these questions regarding their self-concept and invariably choose employers who espouse values that reflect their own. In fact, 56 per cent of Millennials/Zers have "ruled out ever working for a particular organization because of its values or standard of conduct."[47] Compounding this, some Millennials have even gone so far as to put their values ahead of organizational goals. Almost half of Millennials surveyed in the 2016 Deloitte Millennial Survey reported having "chosen not to undertake a task at work because it went against their values or ethics."[48] But how exactly can an organization take steps toward aligning professional and personal purpose? Here are some practical places to start.

Define and Communicate Your Purpose

It is incumbent on an organization to define its purpose, and to define this purpose in a manner that engages Millennials/Zers. Pontefract argues that the purpose of an organization is to "provide service to benefit all intended stakeholders" by delighting its customers, engaging their team members, acting ethically, and using fair practices.[49] There are strong links between *organizational purpose* and *organizational culture*. An engaged and purposeful workforce results in less absenteeism and employee turnover while providing increased productivity and customer satisfaction. BrightHouse, a BCG company, suggests that "employees who derive meaning and purpose from their work, and who are inspired by company leadership, are 2.25 times more productive than satisfied employees" while also enhancing consumer response and passion.[50] We advise organizations to write an organizational declaration of purpose, taking into account all stakeholders, and to communicate it clearly and passionately to those stakeholders.[51]

Shift from Shareholders to Stakeholders

One of the most important dimensions of job satisfaction is one's degree of alignment with their employer's mission.[52] This is especially true for Millennials/Zers; sadly, most feel that most businesses have no purpose beyond making a profit. There are distinct differences in what Millennials/Zers believe the purpose of a business should be and what they perceive it to currently be.[53] In particular, there are five key areas in which Millennials/Zers believe a business's sense of purpose should be focused: providing a good income to employees, being the best possible place to work, improving the skills of employees, providing products and services that make a positive difference to people's lives, and generating and supporting good jobs.[54] Some businesses have picked up on this trend and have, consequently, adapted to accommodate Millennials/Zers in an attempt to attract the best talent. We have seen a shift in some companies from a shareholder model to a one in which stakeholder interests are balanced (dubbed stakeholder balancing).

The stakeholder balancing model focuses to a much higher degree on either those affected by the decisions a corporation makes or its inner communities such as employees, suppliers, customers, government, and even the environmental lobby. This model, which is being increasingly adopted by businesses, considers all parties to be equal in importance to its shareholders; therefore, the interests of these groups are as vital as profit maximization. Millennials/Zers are eager to be part of this model and want to work at companies that embrace it. Stakeholder balancing appeals to their sense of purpose beyond just money and profits – it engages their need to help the world en masse. They want to be part of the vision of a company and to contribute to the company's overall success in the context of society's overall well-being and prosperity.

Make CSR a Priority

The vast majority of Millennials/Zers believe that the success of a business should be measured in terms of more than just its financial performance.[55] Deloitte asked its Millennial Survey respondents: "What are the most important values a business should follow if it is to have long-term success?" The vast majority of respondents suggested that businesses should put employees first and should have a solid foundation of trust and integrity. A significant number of Millennials also mentioned attention to the environment and corporate social responsibility as essential. Very few – only 5 per cent – thought profit-focused values alone would ensure long-term success.[56]

Deloitte also uncovered that societal concerns and ethics are the most common reasons why Millennials change their relationships with businesses.

Forty-two per cent of respondents would be willing to start and deepen a relationship with a business that has products or services that positively impact the environment/society while 38 per cent would stop or reduce their relationship with a business doing the opposite.[57]

Foster Personal Development
This disinterest in merely making a profit, and the need to find a purpose, has led many Millennials/Zers to pursue entrepreneurial careers. The Millennial/Z generations have grown up watching entrepreneurs reach the pinnacle of success before age thirty. Due to this perception, young professionals want a chance to flex their entrepreneurial muscles and view any kind of professional development as a significant advantage. Professional development, or rather skill- building, can, therefore, be used by businesses as a means of fostering commitment in the younger generation.

Millennials/Zers are particularly hungry for opportunities to develop their professional skills. When asked "Who has the most responsibility for preparing workers for Industry 4.0?" 30 per cent of Millennials said business and employers, a higher percentage than those who mentioned educational institutions. Additionally, only one in five respondents believed they had all the skills and knowledge they would need for a world being shaped by Industry 4.0, and 70 per cent said they may only have some or few of the skills required and would need to evolve their own capabilities to increase their value.[58] This implies that Millennials/Zers expect their workplace to provide resources and opportunities to acquire the necessary skills to thrive in industries increasingly adopting digital technologies, such as big data, artificial intelligence, and machine learning.

In the past few years, many organizations have started to tap into this mindset. For example, some are exploring discounted education as an employee benefit.[59] Barclays has started up a young leaders' resource group called Emerge, with the primary goal of helping the company's most recent hires to accelerate their careers through opportunities to develop skills, network, and manage projects through "extracurricular" initiatives inside or outside the company.[60] Similarly, Synchrony, a financial company, has developed and offers placement in its Innovation Stations – collaborative, cross-functional teams across the United States – to encourage high performers to dream up and test bold ideas. BCG allows new hires to do a fellowship in social impact or language learning before their start date, and touts the opportunity to "craft your own journey." Rotational programs as well as internal and external secondments are now common at the management consulting giant. Temporary projects like these are nothing new, but for Millennials/Zers who thrive on challenges, need opportunities to develop their sense of purpose, and have a strong desire to develop professional skills, they are crucial.[61]

Get Creative with Corporate Programs

Millennials/Zers appear to be more loyal to their set of values or ideals than they ever will be to any particular company. This is illustrated in the banking industry, which is experiencing a decline in recruits from America's leading business schools, along with difficulty retaining the Millennials/Zers they do hire. Understanding Millennials/Zers' unique priorities has led to some innovative adaptations in the industry. For example, Citigroup allows new investment-banking analysts to defer starting their jobs for a year to work at a non-profit organization at 60 per cent of their proposed pay. Offering flexibility in this manner gives the employee an invigorated sense of control over their career and a chance to seek a higher purpose in work.

> "Whether I am at work or at school, I need to constantly feel challenged. As soon as I feel too comfortable in what I am doing, I know I am no longer learning and it's time to move on to something new."
> – Austin Doukas, business student, Tulane University (age 21)

Forward-thinking programs that identify high-potential employees and offer them the opportunity to work in other cities are an example of creating purpose. An example from IBM is instructive on how such programs and opportunities should be structured to fully engage Millennials/Zers. IBM used to have a high-potential program that had its top-performing young employees in a classroom for weeks. In 2008, they augmented the classroom experience with opportunities to spend extended periods of time in vastly different parts of the world. Living and working abroad allows employees to gain international exposure and the chance to grow their careers. Called the IBM Corporate Service Corps, IBM high potentials are sent to serve the local communities in the developing world. The program is designed to help "provide IBMers with high-quality leadership development while delivering high-quality problem solving for communities and organizations in emerging markets."[62] During the assignment, participants perform community-driven economic development projects, working at the intersection of business, technology, and society. The Corporate Service Corps offers a triple benefit: leadership development for the IBMers, leadership training and development for the communities, and greater knowledge and enhanced reputation in growth markets for IBM.[63] This program demonstrates how employers should structure professional development programs to engage Millennials/Zers employees on multiple levels: development of professional skills, helping society on a broad scale, and, above all, finding a sense of purpose in their work.

> **❚❚** ❚ think that if you are 24/7 focused just on work, you are actually going to lose your ability to create a vision. I'm not fixated on Fitbit 24/7 – but I think that it is really important that it always be in the back of the mind. That's how great ideas are going to come out."[64]
> – Eric Friedman, CTO, Fitbit

Promote Work-Life Integration

Organizations must make flexibility more than polite talk. Flexibility allows young people the opportunity to maintain a sense of purpose in their personal lives while also being able to expend effort toward excelling and developing a purpose in the professional sphere. They value this genuine blending of their work and personal lives – Millennials/Zers want to lead an integrated lifestyle. If working from home was not the norm for previous generations, Millennials/Zers fully expect this to become common practice. As early as 2013, a study led by oDesk (now Upwork) found that 92 per cent of Millennials want to work remotely and 87 per cent want to work on their own clock, instead of the usual nine-to-five workday.[65] The COVID-19 pandemic has also forced workplaces to finally embrace remote work more fully. Businesses that invested in this kind of flexibility early on are now reaping the benefits and withstanding the storm better than others.

Many Millennials/Zers perceive their parents' generation as one whose lives are riddled with mistakes. The acquisition of a model home, matching BMWs, in-ground pools, and exotic summer holidays outweighed the importance of family for some Moderns. Looking to the future, Millennials/Zers want the opposite of this – they want to integrate their work and family lives before worrying about material success. They are generally less willing to compromise for their jobs for fear of making the same mistakes they feel their parents made. Of course, there are exceptions: investment bankers, lawyers, and consultants, to name just a few, are traditionally viewed as being workaholics and more than familiar with long work hours, often at the expense of family. Consequently, fewer Millennials/Zers are aspiring to fill these positions, primarily due to the lack of balance demanded of those wanting to excel on the job.

However, this desire to integrate work and life extends well past the family and into the desire to find a broader sense of purpose. In this sense, Millennials/Zers want to lead lives outside of work; they want to unplug at the end of the day and spend time on their hobbies and interests. In working with the Millennial generation, I have often heard the 60/80 argument cited: young people want to work 60 per cent of the time while getting paid as if they worked 80 per cent of the time. While I do not feel that this is sustainable, let alone realistic, I do feel that there is room for some renegotiation. To retain top talent, companies will have to negotiate on this basis. For example, Journeys, a leading specialty retailer where young workers make up the majority of the workforce, has created a core time block where all headquarter employees must be in the office unless they are on the road for work. In return, employees are responsible for their results regardless of their work hours and the location from which they work, both of which they are otherwise free to choose based on their lifestyle.

The needs of the Millennial/Zer generations have also been appreciated and accepted by governments and policy-makers. Paternal sabbaticals, for instance, are offered here in Quebec; fathers are welcome to share the parental leave with their spouse after the birth of a child. In 2021 I worked with McKinsey to study fathers who stay home more than two months with newborns: this is appealing to more and more Millennial/Gen Z couples.[66]

Developments at the policy level, which reflect broader social needs, have consequently been embraced in business. At Netflix, for example, an unlimited paternal-leave policy allows employees to spend more time with their newborns and to choose a return date that balances their responsibilities at home and work.[67] The Deloitte Dads, a support group for young working fathers at Deloitte consulting, is another stellar example of change. The company's chief diversity officer has received countless calls from other companies seeking to implement similar programs.[68] Millennial fathers have thus successfully challenged their company culture. All of this is to illustrate that some businesses are paying attention to broader social trends that reflect the needs and desires of the Millennial generation. Businesses must develop an appreciation and accommodation of these needs if they wish to employ and retain the best Millennial, and Gen Z, talent.

I have observed in my considerable years of mentoring that fewer and fewer young people working at world-famous, hyper-demanding firms are willing to spend many years there, as engaging as those businesses can be. This is largely because demanding and inflexible work schedules prevent Millennials/Zers from developing their sense of purpose. When families and too much travel get in the way, they start to hear their inner voice say, "why should you work so hard?" To their credit, firms in the consulting and investment-banking industry are changing their ways to accommodate employees' personal development and fulfillment. Most top consulting firms have their consultants back in their home office on Fridays. They are away only Monday to Thursday, unlike the Sunday-night to Friday-night routine that was once common. McKinsey has introduced a range of flexible, part-time programs, boasting that they have been electing partners who are part-timers for years. Their popular Take Time program offers consultants an unprecedented level of flexibility, whereby employees have pursued a diverse array of personal development projects, including working on a novel, getting advanced scuba certification, and accompanying a spouse on a rural medical residency.[69]

While Millennials/Zers' search for meaning and purpose in their personal and work life might seem challenging for management to accommodate, meeting that need is essential to engage and foster their talent. Indeed, the search for meaning beyond a paycheque is one that many employees, regardless of age, industry, or nationality, are undertaking today.[70] I believe that central to developing a sense of purpose – both on a personal and professional level – is mentorship and guidance. As mentioned at the beginning of this chapter, I am hopeful that Moderns can naturally mentor and connect with Millennials/Zers. In essence, they have much more in common than may be apparent at first glance, even though they are at very different points in their careers. What better way is there for a Millennial/Zer to learn how to integrate life and work than from someone who has already been through this? How businesses and Moderns can effectively foster mentorship relationships in this sense is the subject of the next chapter.

Many boomers appear unwilling, or see themselves as financially unable, to retire at sixty-five or earlier. A famous ad campaign in Canada by insurance giant London Life called Freedom 55 appears not to have been a reality for many boomers – unless they were lucky to have worked for a government and to have a guaranteed and indexed pension. This has caused some consternation among Millennials/Zers and Generation Xers about whether the boomers will ever leave the scene and let them have their day in the sun. Bill Clinton certainly is one boomer who seems not to be accepting the traditional role of ex-presidents to fade into the sunset, though to be honest, he does seem to be doing some good things. Bill Gates also comes to mind as a boomer who has turned from making money and being CEO to making the world a better place through the Bill & Melinda Gates Foundation.[71] Purpose and meaning appeal to all generations. It just may take time for this to kick in for some generations.

8

The Modern Mentor in a
Postmodern Workspace
The Voice of Support

Millennials/Zers have a bad reputation – they are seen as spoiled and lazy workers with high expectations. In a single word, Millennials/Zers are considered to be immature. This is undoubtedly true for some, but I think it to be considerably overstated. To categorically state that all Millennials/Zers are immature is to misunderstand the generation itself. Boomer and Xer managers have a role to play in helping Millennials/Zers outgrow their "immaturity," and that's called mentorship.

Millennials/Zers are unique generations. How they were brought up, what they were taught, and how they think differs markedly from that of older generations. Therefore, they need more effective and adapted forms of mentorship and leadership. In 2020, Millennials formed fully 50 per cent of the global workforce,[1] and they are more numerous than any generation since the soon-to-retire baby boomers (who are retiring in the United States at a rate of about 10,000 a day).[2] It is no longer merely beneficial to mentor these employees; it has become fundamental to the success of any company.

" I was immediately introduced to different mentors who provided continuous feedback not only in relation to their expectations for me, but also in the context of my own goals and values. It was through this diverse support that they built a positive environment to learn in."
– Liam Timmins, intern, Accenture Ottawa (age 24)

" Millennials/Zers have a different work ethic. There's an interest in working off-site sometimes. It's a shift from our generation or my generation where there seemed to be more of an ability to roll up your sleeves, work hard, and hope or expect that things would come. Millennials/Zs want to know what's coming first, and then they will do the hard work if it aligns with their values."
– Julian Giacomelli, president and CEO, rise Kombucha

Millennials/Zers and Mentoring

Mentoring is an essential part of Millennials/Zers' conception of their career. According to a Virtual Survey, they "think mentoring is the most effective and most desired type of career development training."[3]

When mentoring Millennials/Zers, a different approach is needed than the traditional understanding most Boomers are comfortable with. An article in the *Wall Street Journal* a while ago suggested that "the traditional mentoring arrangement just doesn't work anymore. A single, senior colleague can't possibly keep up with all the changes in the fast-moving world of work."[4] Millennials/Zers, therefore, "generally aren't satisfied with corporate training programs, including mentoring opportunities." They view these programs as being "very awkward and forced."[5]

Millennials/Zers have a reputation for being "attention sponges,"[6] always craving and demanding the attention and approval of their colleagues and mentors. "They crave – and respond to – a good, positive coach who can make all the difference in their success."[7] This means that traditional forms of mentoring, while ideal for the boomer generation, may lead to frustration and wasted effort if applied directly to Millennials/Zers. They value "honest, timely and useful coaching" and place an extremely high premium on a manager who will "give straight feedback."[8]Millennials/Zers expect their mentors to assist them with achieving their accelerated ambitions. This can be attributed to the fact that Millennials have, as a *Harvard Business Review* article outlines, "been working on their resumes practically since they were toddlers because there are so many of them and so few (relatively speaking) spots at top schools and top companies."[9] Millennials/Zers want "a road map to success, and they expect their companies to provide it."[10] Business schools understand this need and arrange mentorship opportunities (even for undergraduates). McGill, for example, pairs students with mentors in their field and geographic area of interest to begin mentorship even before entering the workforce. Programs like these of course heighten the expectations that Millennials/Zers have of their employers upon graduation. With the decline in company loyalty among Millennials/Zers, organizations must foster a sense of corporate loyalty in Millennials/Zers to increase retention; this can be done through mentorship. Millennials/Zers need to know that support and professional development are available at their company, and in a format that they can understand and benefit from.

Crucial to the success of mentorship programs is the ability to recognize Millennials/Zers' unique needs and wants within the workplace – significantly different from those of previous generations.[11] Most Millennials/Zers have grown up in sheltered and supportive environments, and they're looking for similar conditions in the workplace. Many believe that success is determined by the strength of the collective as opposed to that of the individual, and they want collaboration instead of isolation.[12] One of the key responsibilities of managers is to surround the Millennial/Gen Zer with a great team that, when working together, can make a difference.[13]

In this sense, the manager's job is not simply to oversee the completion and quality of their work but more "to coach [the Millennial] while they are the most fragile, rather than fostering a 'sink or swim' environment."[14] Millennials want "to feel like they are part of a community at work – nearly 9 in 10 want a workplace to be social and fun."[15] Managers must, therefore, ensure that the team setting caters to the Millennial/Zer, especially when they first begin work. This is essential to fostering the Millennial/Zer's development and is crucial to the business capitalizing fully on the Millennial/Zer's skills. Studies have recognized that "newcomers are fragile and malleable, and a little boost can go a long way toward reducing anxiety and improving performance."[16] Mentors and mentorship programs become especially crucial in this context because "transitions are a particularly good time to seek out a mentor ... whether you are making a career change, taking on a new role, or contemplating leaving a job, advice from someone who has done it before can be helpful."[17]

Millennials/Zers "grew up with social media and texting, but they can also be highly isolated in 'real-life' because of overreliance on technology for communication."[18] Experts have indicated that this has led to "poor people skills, low emotional intelligence and an inability to handle interpersonal challenges."[19] Millennials/Zers may, therefore, crave one-on-one relationships, especially in the form of guidance through a new work environment. They, therefore, view mentors as meaningful contributors to their personal growth and "sometimes expect mentors to tell them what to do" flat out.[20] Millennials/Zers consider their mentors to be confidantes – wiser individuals who can guide them.

To truly understand Millennials/Zers, it is necessary to understand the roots of their psychological and sociological behaviour. A blog post on *The Muse* indicates the causal roots of these trends and shows, from a Millennial/Zer's perspective, the need for tailored mentorship in their careers.[21] The author starts by suggesting that Millennials/Zers have come of age during a time of "massive uncertainty" and have been "uniquely, dramatically shaped by the major events of the New Millennium," including globalization, 9/11, and the Great Recession. This has led Millennials/Zers to feel that they "have no reason to trust institutions, and that goes for employers as well."[22]

Secondly, Millennials/Zers are, as is widely known, "conditioned to expect constant feedback" due to the constant stream of feedback received during their formative years; this can sometimes "border on the unreasonable." Finally, and perhaps most importantly in the context of this chapter, Millennials/Zers sense the antipathy of their employers and measure themselves against their peers' successes. The author notes that Millennials, subconsciously, "measure [them]selves against [their] parents' generation, and against one another." They are incredibly ambitious, but at the same time, they can feel lost and alone as if they "haven't figured [them]selves out yet." As the author concludes, "Millennials need older generations to adopt and mentor us in the workplace."[23]

> "[M]illennials] are hypersensitive and they crave feedback. There's a desire to be brought into what we're doing, and to be told the big picture of how it all fits in. One of the biggest areas of feedback that I get, and I have to remind myself, is 'where do they all fit in?'"
> – Rob Khazzam, general manager, Uber Canada

Ultimately, it is essential to improve Millennial/Z employees' loyalty and commitment to their organization. This requires a restructuring of mentorship. Consequently, organizations have adapted their mentorship strategies and programs to accommodate what Millennials/Zers expect and need from mentors and mentorship compared to previous generations. The following is an analysis of the differences, and the strategies that companies can use to accommodate Millennials/Zers in light of these differences.

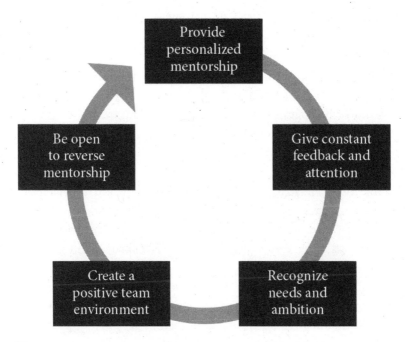

Figure 8.1
Cycle of commitments for successful mentoring of Millennials/Zers

Differences in Mentoring Millennials/Zers

The mentoring landscape has changed enormously in the last few decades. For example, Millennials/Zers tend to have multiple mentors, including traditional older managers and peer mentors. Also, mentorship has emerged as a two-way road. Boomers and Xers need to embrace these new approaches to be effective mentors. Unfortunately, studies have shown that "while mentoring has morphed, our collective thinking on it has not and many held-over myths still prevail."[24] The result is a considerable gap between the way businesses implement mentorship programs and what Millennials/Zers expect, need, and want from their mentors.

A primary cause of this divergence is that Millennials/Zers desire consistent feedback; they are hungry for great mentors who are willing to put in the time, accept multiple mentees, and be reverse mentored. Because of the constant coaching and feedback received throughout their formative years, Millennials/ Zers likely view their mentors as parental figures or teachers, rather than in the traditional role of employer or boss. This perception has drastically shifted what Millennials/Zers expect from mentorship programs and their attitudes toward traditional mentorship programs.

Mentorship programs were traditionally set up by human resources departments, with young employees being partnered with executives. This approach is increasingly being rejected by Millennials/Zers who "are disrupting that mentorship model." Experts have indicated that, rather than looking for a simple mentorship relationship, Millennials are "in pursuit of a sponsor, the preferred academic term for a mentor who goes beyond advising to actively promoting the underling." Studies have shown that "sponsorship can be effective for securing better compensation, faster promotions, and job satisfaction." Millennials/Zers are looking to get more than simple advice and information from their mentors. As opposed to passively accepting traditional models, "they want better, faster and more effective mentorship programs – or they're ditching HR and doing it on their own."

Interestingly, as mentioned previously, Millennials/Zers do not rely on only one mentor. More and more, the notion of a 'perfect mentor' is being abandoned. This is, again, likely related to the constant need for feedback and validation. Millennials/Zers surround themselves with a network of coaches; many Millennials/Zers "have several advisors they turn to" throughout their careers, for issues both major and minor. According to Monica Higgins, a professor at Harvard's Graduate School of Education, "one senior person can no longer be the only place your turn for career support."[25] Younger people seek short-term, informal relationships that avoid interrupting each other's day-to-day lives.

The terms "mentorship" and "mentor" are increasingly being replaced with notions such as the "developmental network ... the handful of people you can go to for advice and who you trust to have your best interests in mind."[26] Millennials/Zers are used to searching for and identifying their mentors; they may often feel that "it can be helpful to get a variety of perspectives on an issue"[27] rather than just one "right" or "best" opinion. They feel that "one senior person can no longer be the only place [they] turn to for support" and are accordingly "less respectful of more experienced colleagues and don't feel compelled to follow in the same path as their superiors."[28] Mandatory corporate mentorship programs – that often bring about such advice – often feel forced and unauthentic. While a mentor might seem ideal on paper, Millennials/Zers find it difficult to connect with an individual who they do not personally deem relevant.

Millennials/Zers are active in many different forums, such as professional networks, volunteer organizations, and social media. A recent survey notes that most Millennials/Zers "like to network outside of their organizations," and companies must accommodate this desire, although it may seem foreign to many. Millennials/Zers often form mentorships "outside of the corporate walls via social networks, events or external programs."[29] The online world of LinkedIn, for example, provides immediate access to industry professionals from around the world. Unfortunately, not all social media initiatives result in happy endings.

With the rise of social media, "giving and receiving mentoring tips doesn't have to take a lot of time,"[30] and new social media innovations can be used to streamline, expedite, and enhance the mentoring experience for Millennials/Zers. No longer does the notion that "mentoring is a formal long-term relationship" apply. In fact, "a long-term advising relationship may be unrealistic and unnecessary"[31] simply because Millennials/Zers' career preferences and objectives change so frequently. This stands in stark contrast to the mentoring relationships of the past and is something that both businesses and business leaders must adapt to.

However, not everything from traditional mentorship relationships needs to fade away into the ether of this new technological era. By dedicating resources to mentoring in the manner preferred by Millennials/Zers, companies can retain these employees and earn their loyalty by encouraging them to "become the leaders in the organization when their predecessors retire or move on to other opportunities." Companies must realize that the "more [they] invest (fiscally and emotionally) in young workers, the more likely it is they'll become engaged in [the] organization's mission."

The following are some mentoring strategies tailored to the unique Millennial/Gen Z perspective that will enable you to respond to the specific challenges of better integrating them into your team.

Reverse Mentoring

Many organizations are currently struggling to solve the problem of Millennial retention. Like many business leaders, you may have asked yourself: "what do we need to do to help them be loyal to our firm?" Introducing meaning into their work,[32] mentoring them, and trusting them to do more are all great first steps. That being said, I believe that to truly integrate Millennials/Zers into your teams and to fully benefit from that integration, the introduction of a systematic *reverse mentorship program* is essential. This approach is not entirely new; in the late 1990s, General Electric's Jack Welch used reverse mentoring to have junior people teach senior executives about the Internet,[33] something seemingly beyond the boomers at the time, but a breeze for the younger generation. Today's reverse mentoring extends far beyond just sharing knowledge about technology; today's programs include how senior executives think about strategic issues and leadership, and the mindset with which they approach their work.[34] Reverse mentoring, done well, can result in better-aligned strategies with a turbulent world and more implementable strategies for the whole organization.

What Is It and What Are the Key Benefits?

Unlike regular mentoring, where there is a top-down flow of information from the manager to the employee,[35] reverse mentoring flips the script and encourages information flow from the employee to the manager. This is especially interesting in the context of Millennials/Zers, who can provide valuable insights because they understand emerging technologies and social media trends (among other things) in a way that their older counterparts do not. "From the outside, it is often assumed that mentorship is about youth who want business experience, and about telling them what to do. In reality, people of any age can be mentored. It is less about telling someone what to do and more about empowering the mentee to make their own decisions."[36] Mentoring, in this sense, is "not a one-sided arrangement in which the mentor provides only guidance."[37] Instead, it is a mutually reinforcing relationship where both sides benefit. I am undoubtedly mentored by the several undergrads who work for me in any given year. I mentor them more than they mentor me, but unlike ten years ago, there is no question in my mind that I am reverse mentored regularly by them, too. A rough rule of thumb is that most of them mentor me 20 to 25 per cent of the time; of course, some more and some a little less. In the business world, when I give talks to groups of executives, I tell them, if you are not being reverse mentored at least 15 per cent of the time, you are a jerk.[38]

While many of us have benefitted from listening to our younger peers for decades,[39] there is a marked benefit today more than in the past to purposefully setting aside time to learn from Millennial employees. They may talk to you about sustainability and the importance of reducing the presence of single-use plastic. Or advocate how business must take on board a stakeholder, not just shareholder, view.[40] Or introduce you to a new piece of technology, or even share the latest social media trends with you. In a recent CEO Insights class at McGill, a very senior businessperson in his fifties told us that he got most of his news from TikTok. The twenty-something MBAS and I looked at each other in astonishment! While this may seem a small detail, shifts such as these are not the only difference between a business that actively integrates Millennials/Zers within its teams and one that does not. It may also be the difference between an organization that evolves, and one that ceases to be successful in today's quickly changing world. By broadening the range of sources that you receive information from, you are opening yourself up to new opportunities for learning. The learning that Millennials/Zers can share with you is invaluable – and as a boomer who is frequently mentored by his students, I have seen this happen often.

A *Harvard Business Review* article by Jennifer Jordan and Michael Sorell outlined the many benefits of implementing a reverse mentoring program, but three are particularly significant.[41] First and foremost: there is a massive benefit to employee retention, something that will benefit your firm not just when it comes to Millennials/Zers but also when Generation Z begins to play a more significant role in the workforce. A stark example that Jordan and Sorell give of these trends comes in the form of the bank BNY Mellon, which set up an extensive reverse mentoring program to address its retention problems. They experienced a staggering 96 per cent retention rate for the first cohort of Millennial mentors and decided to make this program a staple of their employee value proposition. This increased retention will benefit your teams not only in the short run, since you won't always have to be replacing and retraining members who leave, but also in the long term, with employees who are dedicated to your team and your business.

Second, reverse mentoring provides specific opportunities for Millennials/ Zers to share their digital skills with you. From showing you new features to teaching you new pieces of technology, their digital savvy is a well of knowledge that should not go untapped. The vast majority of these employees grew up with technology and, hence, do not share the same aversion to it as some of us do. When I say this, I don't mean to make you feel like a dinosaur – I say this to encourage you to go to your Millennial employees and learn from them. Not only will they be happier at the end of the exchange, because they will feel like a trusted and contributing member of the team, but you and your business will benefit from the shared knowledge.

Reverse mentoring is a real driver of culture change. With Millennials/Zers being so in touch with their peers through social media and other pieces of tech, they are acutely aware of some of the shifts that are happening in the world around us. Their interconnectedness enables them to do research in a way that none of us really can: they can ask several hundred or more of their friends for their thoughts in a nearly instantaneous manner. While this might seem like a relatively benign fact, this could be hugely helpful for your business. Think of all the companies that are currently struggling to re-establish their image after circulating publicity campaigns that were deemed insensitive, or after taking their business in the wrong direction. If these businesses had had opportunities to test out these ideas during reverse mentoring meetings, I believe some of those missteps could have been avoided altogether.

For the last twelve years, I have taken forty McGill students somewhere in the world on what is called the Hot Cities of the World Tour. The trip's slogan is: "Taking the future to the future," that is, taking undergraduates to where the world's economy is growing rapidly. In 2023 our trip is to Ghana and the Ivory Coast. Every year I have two undergraduate students help me organize the trip. In the fall semester, I sit down with them and say we each get a vote. I tell them that they can outvote me because I want the view of the majority of the people on the trip – the undergraduates – to be important. They understand the world of undergraduates far better than I do, and I want them to not only own the trip but also make sure it is designed with undergraduates in mind (while abiding by the university's regulations, of course). This is powerful, useful, and very helpful reverse mentoring by students who are twenty or twenty-one years of age.

Third, reverse mentoring can be an incredibly positive force for diversity in the workplace.[42] While many of us are (and should be) pushing for increased diversity in our workplaces, it can sometimes be difficult to understand the perspective of minorities and the changes that would truly benefit them.[43] Reverse mentoring provides a platform for these questions to be discussed and addressed. Millennials/Zers form an incredibly diverse generation, and Generation Z is predicted to be the most diverse ever. This point of leverage is already important, but it will become essential – and reverse mentoring can help you address it effectively.

How Can You Benefit from It?

While the principle behind reverse mentoring is a relatively simple one, the introduction of such a program can be tricky, given how different it is from traditional "mentoring channels." To ensure the eventual success of your reverse mentoring program, it is important to be aware of a few pitfalls before telling all C-suite members that they have to find a Millennial mentor.[44]

Firstly – and literally most importantly – the right match is essential. While this may seem obvious, it is worth emphasizing up front. Much like a regular mentor-mentee relationship, finding the right match is a difficult but crucial part of the process. But, unlike a regular mentor-mentee relationship, where the employer-employee relationship is already established, a reverse mentoring completely shifts pre-established narratives. Hence, it relies in no small measure on the mentor and mentee managing to create a bond. Without their sharing an initial bond, or if they lack compatibility, their exchanges will not be productive. Let me put it this way: setting up your most extroverted head of sales with the quietest Millennial may not lead to as much learning on the part of either.

While an initial bond is indeed important for the mentorship, don't be afraid to move even further outside your comfort zone when being paired with a mentee. Reverse mentorship will have its awkward moments at the start, and to minimize these types of encounters with your mentee, you may be tempted to work with Millennials or Gen Zers who are quite similar to you. However, don't underestimate the value of diverse partnerships. According to a March 2022 *Financial Times* article by Heather McGregor, executive dean of Edinburgh Business School at Heriot-Watt University, diversity in mentorships can reap substantial benefits for both the mentor and the mentee. McGregor cites UK credit management company Lowell as a successful example of such an initiative. Members of the executive committee were paired with earlier-career employees from under-represented groups, such as women, people from different ethnic backgrounds, or single parents. In reflecting on these experiences, some executives valued the mentorship, remarking that it "really helped ... to put into perspective the decisions you might make."[45] Such value-generating mentorships can help managers to understand not only the experiences of a younger employee but also those of someone with different lived experiences.

Other successful reverse mentors include Jack Welch, a pioneer of reverse mentorship at General Electric over twenty years ago when he introduced the program to help employees become more familiar with the Internet. Welch sought to pair senior employees with younger, tech-savvy employees under the age of twenty-five. From this initiative came the backbone and philosophy of reverse mentorship: stepping outside of one's comfort zone and putting aside one's seniority in order to learn something new. Consumer group Estée Lauder also has an established reverse mentorship program. The company touts itself as a "learning organization," sharing insights both externally with partners and internally among employees. Their CEO Global Reverse Mentor Program was established in 2015 and pairs senior leaders with Millennial and Gen Z employees so that they can learn from one another. According to the company, it "allows rising talent at the company to share valuable insights and perspectives, as well as connect trends to leaders' priority topics."[46] In other words, for an organization like Estée Lauder, reverse mentorship plays a key role in helping more senior managers grow their business and keep it relevant with the times. Younger minds can often help to bring a fresh perspective and can serve as a link to the very people you may be trying to cater to.

Secondly, you must ensure the Modern mentees have a strong commitment to the program. These programs can only truly work once both mentors and Postmodern mentees commit to it, and the novelty factor for mentors makes it likely they will adhere to it without needing much convincing. Mentees on the other hand – who are managers and C-suite members like yourself – may need a little more convincing to truly commit themselves to such a program and to go to their mentoring sessions with an open heart and open mind.

Some skepticism about the usefulness of these sessions is natural and will likely occur initially with a majority of your participants. Framing these sessions in a way that does not allow skepticism to hinder early progress, or prevent the mentees from seeing the benefits of the activity, is absolutely essential. Actively encouraging them to participate – and give it their best – will pay dividends down the line.

Thirdly, you must address the potential fear and distrust on the part of mentees. Many executives and managers are fearful of revealing their lack of digital aptitude or knowledge of contemporary issues to their employees. This tendency can greatly hinder the productivity of reverse mentoring sessions. As part of convincing the Gen Zers to commit to the program, it is essential that you also ensure that they go to these meetings having shed their doubts and fears about opening themselves up to their boomer and Xer managers. Quite clearly, and as you know from your instances of mentoring, it is tough to mentor someone who is unwilling to open up. Mentees should reflect on this trend before starting this process, enabling them to go into these meetings without fear of opening up to their Millennial mentors.

Lastly, one should not mix a shadow board, that is a group of younger, more junior employees that works with senior executives on strategic initiatives, and a reverse mentoring program.[47] While shadow boards are another interesting way to integrate Millennials/Zers into your teams and workplace, they are a fundamentally different initiative than reverse mentoring programs, and one should not be mistaken for the another. Companies that have tried to introduce both programs to a single cohort have suffered from one program winning out and the other being left by the wayside, with those opportunities for learning and growth lost as well. If you wish to introduce both programs, you could follow Estée Lauder's lead and use different participants for each program. This would enable you to benefit from both initiatives, while not jeopardizing the success of either.

Alternative Mentoring Strategies

Another key strategy that is becoming increasingly popular is *speed mentoring* in which "aspiring mentees face-off individually with prospective mentors, speed dating style, for short bursts of advice and a cache of business cards."[48]

This strategy has been adopted by academic institutions such as the University of Texas at Austin and organizations such as New York Women in Communications. This strategy engages Millennials/Zers' need for more than one mentor and, ultimately, allows them to get a diverse array of advice and information in a short period of time. This strategy is perhaps familiar to Millennials/Zers for its similarity to social media; speed mentoring can be compared to the plethora of connections and information received on Twitter or Facebook.

Strategies for Optimizing Mentorship

Mentors cultivate the future generations of leaders. Moderns should and must fill these shoes with incoming employees, not only to instill company loyalty among Millennials/Zers but also to benefit older generations. Following are three aspects to keep in mind as you continue to mentor your Millennials/Zers.

Encourage Millennials/Zers to Step Up to More Responsibility

Millennials/Zers are incredibly ambitious. They desire responsibility and opportunities to validate themselves. They need to understand that they, too, bear responsibility for maintaining a fruitful mentorship relationship. For Millennials/Zers, successful businesses not only make money but also make the world a better place. Employers must provide Millennials/Zers with opportunities and responsibilities that allow them to feel engaged in their mentorship relationship and fulfilled in their work.

Reverse mentoring can be used as a key strategy that enables Millennials/Zers to both link their work with the more strategic work done by upper management and find meaning in their work. It allows them to play a useful role in helping upper management make decisions that are key to the workplace. They can feel that they are contributing to the overarching business by sharing knowledge of technology and social media with upper management. Giving Millennials/Zers responsibility and input into the organization at large also meets their needs and desires; it may make them feel less like a cog and more like they have made a genuine impact on the company they work for. The key is to get Millennials/Zers involved and make them feel included.

Demonstrate the Characteristics of a Strong Leader

By engaging in mentoring, leaders will come to understand Millennials/Zers – and that is the first step in effectively leading them. By coming to better understand and accommodate Millennials/Zers' views, opinions, and visions, business leaders will be cultivating the generation that will follow in their footsteps. Real business leaders will embrace alternative mentoring strategies and customize their leadership style to their Millennial employees, the future of the workforce.

However, leadership in this context goes beyond simply tailoring mentoring programs to accommodate Millennials/Zers' views and needs. It goes directly to the quality of mentoring, and Millennials/Zers expect to be inspired by their mentors. As mentioned above, Millennials/Zers prefer for their work to be centred on causes they believe in, which allows them to feel they are making a difference in the world. Millennials/Zers see the role of a leader, and thus a mentor, as "providing a vision, enhancing a relationship and serving as a principled role model … [and] to a lesser degree, being enthusiastic and being an expert also matters." In this sense, business leaders must be cautious and wary in the way they present themselves to Millennials/Zers in mentorship contexts; ultimately, every behaviour of a leader matters and the little efforts add up over time.

Closely related to this is the concept of authenticity, as discussed in chapter 6. To effectively lead and mentor Millennials/Zers, business leaders must be authentic. Millennials/Zers demand "an approachable manager and a role model whom they can emulate."[49] It is, therefore, crucial to be authentic, lest you lose the confidence of a Millennial mentee and employee.

Engage in Formal and Ad-hoc, Positive and Negative Feedback

Mentorship programs must validate Millennials/Zers' need for a constant stream of feedback (more on this, and how best to provide it, in chapter 9). These generations are hard-wired, from their upbringing, to require continuous feedback on their performance, and relentless validation of their work. Feedback is vital, and something that this generation loves. In the next chapter, I discuss the four reasons why they do and give some practical advice on how to provide feedback to Millennials/Zers.

On the whole, successful mentors accept the generational needs of Millennials/Zers. They hold regular meetings, highlight noteworthy actions, and provide constructive criticism. They know that there can never be enough clarity. True leadership, in this sense, involves ensuring that mentoring programs are not only available and tailored to Millennials/Zers' unique needs but also a truly valuable experience to both the organization and the mentee. At the end of the day, Millennials/Zers want you to take notice. Rather than fighting them, why not join them? It can be a win-win situation for all parties. The future of every company lies in the ability of their Millennials/Zers to succeed. To be a great leader, one must also be a great mentor. So why not step up to the plate?

9

The Millennial/Zer Need for Feedback
Four Reasons Why and How to Give It

Millennials/Zers love feedback. They will approach you for it at every opportunity. Why, you may ask? One of my research associates, Gareth Craze, looked into what research suggests and concluded four key reasons why Postmoderns love and need, what appears to be, *constant* feedback. Following discussion of those reasons, and based on solid research, this chapter offers some of the latest thinking on useful feedback.

Perhaps one of the more prominent aspects of feedback that both business academics and Millennials/Zers themselves have focused on is the way that Millennials/Zers receive feedback. While constant feedback is their expectation, there is now a steadily growing body of evidence to support the tailoring of feedback delivery mechanisms to the Millennial/Gen Z needs, values, and mindset.[1] As detailed throughout this book, an individual's worldview and cultural lens will almost always affect their social interactions and relationships – including those in the workplace.[2] This applies to generational differences and, in this context, it seems evident that the nature and delivery of feedback needs to change to be more valuable and productive. Feedback must be adapted to the Millennial mindset, not only in the way it is delivered but also how frequently it is delivered.[3]

What Moderns must understand, above all, is that as far as Millennials/Zers are concerned, feedback is not a luxury – they *depend* on it. Millennials/Zers have grown up with constant feedback and positive reinforcement; they have adapted to using this as a dependable source of information about themselves.[4] It is essential to their self-concept and self-reflection. Without it, they are lost.

In the next part of this chapter, I focus on the four distinct influences that have shaped this generational phenomenon: *parental, peer/social, educational,* and *technological*. Each demands its own specific considerations when looking to develop sensible and effective feedback systems in the workplace. Overall, the Millennials/Zers' imperative for feedback must be appreciated and furnished by businesses in order to engage and develop their talent.

Parental Influence

Millennials were the first generation to be driven around with the "Baby on Board" bumper sticker. This is a vivid symbol of the shift in parenting style, where the child became the central focus for many families. Understanding Millennials' upbringing is one of the keys to explaining their desire to be listened to, regardless of what they may lack in experience.

The first, and perhaps the overarching and most influential, factor in the lives of Millennials/Zers is their parents. The context in which Moderns grew up significantly impacted their parenting style, and therefore influenced the social norms and attitudes instilled in Millennials/Zers during their childhood. Moderns were raised by parents who grew up in times of relative austerity, with a predominant societal emphasis on grit and hard work. However, as they entered the workforce, they began to embrace the benefits of having a work-life integration.[5] During the childhood of their Millennial children, Moderns were able to enjoy relatively prosperous lives, the result of success that came from an upbringing based on stoicism and the value of a good work ethic.

> "Millennials/Zers have less grit and resiliency."
> – Frank Kollmar, president and CEO, L'Oreal Canada

The prosperity of this era encouraged material consumption, enabling Millennials/Zers to have fun, luxurious childhoods – teeming with Game Boys, Furbys, and Pokémon – quite different from those of their parents. More importantly, the influx of wealth and prosperity allowed many of their Modern parents to spend more time focused on their children, attending to their needs on all fronts, placing a great deal of emphasis on individual differentiation and child-centric parenting.[6] The extreme form of this is what some colloquially refer to as "helicopter parenting." While this description may seem

Figure 9.1
Bumper sticker symbolizing
parenting shift in rearing
of Millennials

contradictory to the image of the boomer parent shared in chapter 6 – as figures who answered only to The Man, sacrificing work-life balance and meaningful contact with their children – it's important to hold both of these notions
in hand simultaneously. The identity of the Modern parent was shaped
through their hard work, yet the successes they enjoyed enabled them to com-
pensate by being ultra-focused on their offspring. Millennial children sat at
the apex of this contradiction: having parents who were simultaneously absent
and desperate to be fully involved in their lives at the same time.

As a result of these trends, Millennials/Zers grew up in an unprecedented
era of receiving specific feedback regarding their development: praise for excelling and corrective feedback for improvement. A large part of their formative education consisted of a reliably perpetual stream of feedback that served
as a barometer of their progress and ability to achieve their goals.

This has significant implications for the future of the workplace. Baby
boomers entered the workforce – and built the current business environment

– coloured by the values of stoicism and self-reliance that reflected their up-bringing by the Depression generation. Their children, the Millennials/Zers, by contrast, are building the future of the business world from a mindset that sees purposeful praise and constructive criticism as a primary motivator. They view consistent and continuous on-demand feedback as a fundamentally desirable – in fact, necessary – means of promoting self-improvement.[7] The idea of having performance reviews only on a yearly or quarterly basis is a strange departure from what has come to intuitively define the lives of Millennials/Zers.[8] As children, they were raised to expect constant feedback, and as adults, they expect no less from their supervisors in the workplace. The era of the annual performance review should be dead and gone!

Peer/Social Influence

Beyond their immediate family (due to frequent moves for career, the influence of the extended family is much reduced), peers are a tremendous influence on Millennials/Zers.[9] Millennials/Zers are more likely to define themselves in relation to their peers; their behaviours and values are more likely to be defined by the social norms that are characteristic of their own generation's zeitgeist.[10] When baby boomers were teenagers, their peer group was largely homogeneous. Given the social mores and relative conservatism during the childhood of most Moderns, diversity was more rare. This stands in stark contrast to the high level of diversity that is taken for granted by Millennials/ Zers.

"We now see Millennial men spending more on cosmetics than a lot of women."
– Frank Kollmar, president and CEO, L'Oreal Canada

The counterculture and civil rights movements, among other paradigm-shifting cultural phenomena, that characterized the adult years of most Moderns set the groundwork for Millennials/Zers' tolerant attitudes. They embraced diversity and thereby broadened their potential social circle and the scope of their peer network. Additionally, gender norms have become more fluid.

This expansion in both the size and diversity of Millennials/Zers' peer circles increased the influence of peer perspectives on Millennials/Zers as a generation.[11] Add to this the vast global interconnectedness created by the Internet revolution – from which even the eldest Millennials/Zers have benefitted since their adolescence – and the result is a generation influenced more than ever by the perspectives of their peer network.[12] The rise of social media has only increased the magnitude of this effect.

The influence of peers has tremendous implications for the manner in which Millennials/Zers effectively receive feedback. The old dynamic of feedback from superior to subordinate is strikingly at odds with what Millennials/Zers have come to expect and need, which is more in line with feedback known as "360-degree" – from co-workers and hierarchical equals as well as superiors. Similarly relevant is the fact that Millennials/Zers have been raised, more so than any previous generation, to value, appreciate, and encourage all contributions from all contributors, regardless of status or position.[13] Peer feedback is seen as an honest and relevant means of identifying one's strengths and shortcomings. While standing among peers has always been of importance in the workplace, for the Millennial generation, the peer dynamic and feedback from peers can serve as a call-to-arms to be a valuable contributor to a group whose members' opinions they highly value, and who they often judge their performance against.[14] For this reason, peer feedback can be used to mobilize and engage with a Millennial workforce, perhaps even more so than feedback from direct superiors.

Educational Influence

The context in which Millennials/Zers were educated has also had significant impacts on their mindset and has reinforced their need for feedback. Due to the unique parenting style of Moderns, teachers and educators of Millennials/Zers were charged with caring for a generation that had been nurtured with regular praise and corrective feedback. The 1980s and '90s thus saw an increasing focus on the individual student of the classroom, rather than the class as a whole, emphasizing instead each child's individual needs and abilities.[15] This caused several shifts in teaching methodology and interaction styles with students in the classroom: increased attentiveness to the unique strengths of each child; focused monitoring and positive reinforcement on their progress in each subject; and immediate feedback where they needed improvement, often involving their parents.[16] How feedback has changed from the days of cumulative final exams! Stone and Heen in their book, *Thanks for the Feedback*, estimate that a schoolchild in the United States will be handed back as many as 300 assignments, papers, and tests in a single year.[17]

Millennials/Zers, in contrast to Moderns, place an especially high importance on the value of education.[18] Illustrating this, Stone and Heen point out that almost two million teenagers take the SAT (Scholastic Aptitude Test) exam each year. This isn't to suggest that previous generations didn't value or appreciate education. Rather, it is to say that for Millennials/Zers, academic achievement is intimately tied to internalized notions of personal ability in a way that wasn't the case for previous generations. A commonly heard expression on campus is "a master's is the new bachelor's."[19] Being educated at merely the high school – or even the undergraduate – level is viewed less as a predictor of vocational success and more as a given. This means that Millennials/Zers have effectively been bombarded by feedback given within educational institutions for the majority of their lives. No longer merely an indicator of achievement or success, feedback is relied upon for guidance, direction, and affirmation in their lives.

The upshot of this trend is that this emphasis on education, in addition to fostering a need for constant feedback, is seen by Millennials/Zers as a continuous lifelong process. They believe in continuous educational improvement to provide accurate information about how to better manage their relative strengths and weaknesses over time. For Millennials/Zers, it is not enough to just be told *where* they are excelling or falling short – they have to be shown *how* they are succeeding or failing and *how* they must, or can continue to, improve. In short, they need to be *educated*, and any feedback they receive in the workplace should take this into account.[20]

Technological Influence

The influence of technology is perhaps what most sets Millennials/Zers apart from previous generations. This includes both stark differences in computer literacy and disparities in access to technology. In most developed nations, most of even the oldest Millennials/Zers already had significant computer literacy skills while in elementary school. By the time the youngest Millennials/Zers were in high school, the Internet and social media were an essential part of their lives. The Pew Research Center, in conjunction with the Berkman Center for Internet & Society at Harvard, conducted a national survey of

American youth in early 2013.[21] They found that almost half of the students below the age of eleven have access to smart devices, smartphones, laptops, or tablets. When expanded for ages between eleven to eighteen years, this trend holds and even shows significant increases in the usage of such devices. Almost 90 per cent of the students in this age range have access to smartphones; nearly 50 per cent have access to tablets.[22] This can be easily compared to Moderns who, if lucky, would have had access to only a computer and, at

> **"This** generation is so bright and connected. They think globally, they are more agile and tech savvy."
> – Paul Desmarais Jr, chairman and CO-CEO, Power Corporation of Canada

best, limited Internet access at home. This survey is from their youth, some seven years before the publication of this book, and it shows how they were at this even in their preteen years.

Due to their ready availability and quick access, technology and social media are being increasingly used by Millennials/Zers to make everyday decisions. According to a research study on marketing to Millennials/Zers from the consumer and retail group at Market Strategies International, Millennial consumers are nearly three times as likely as other generations to use social media as a research tool before they make a purchase.[23] In chapter 3, we even saw the Millennial tendency to self-diagnose before seeing a doctor. This immediate and rapid availability of information via the Internet and social media in the retail context has similar implications for the workplace in terms of feedback.

Millennials/Zers expect to receive feedback not only instantaneously, the way information is received from social media, but also from a diverse array of sources. This is tied intrinsically to the discussion of the trends detailed above. It is also useful to consider the fact that Millennials/Zers are increasingly using multiple outlets of social media. Ubiquitous and rapid access to technology has changed how Millennials/Zers interact with each other and the world, totally changing the paradigm of how they perceive the world and how the world perceives them.

Aside from the mass global and informational connectivity available to Millennials/Zers for most of their lives, they have spent considerably more time than Moderns interacting with computers.[24] Despite the impersonal nature of computer-mediated interactions, for Millennials/Zers, these interactions have served as an incredibly reliable provider of feedback; at times,

" My experience of Millennials/Zers is that they have a different frame of reference than the generation before. The Millennial frame of reference is around social media and the World Wide Web. It is a fundamentally different reference point compared to prior generations."
– Bishop Riscylla Shaw, Anglican Church of Canada

technology and social media can serve as a sort of surrogate parent, peer, or educator.[25] In this context, one specific fact must be kept in mind: most computer software, and even social media in some cases, is not bound up in emotional considerations and does not project (or mimic) the emotional intelligence that might engender the absence of honesty or cushion the "harsh truth" in human interaction. Technology generally deals in right and wrong, and black and white, not in shades of grey. Thus, technological interactions, unlike personal interactions, rarely hold any information back for the supposed benefit of the user. They are, for better or worse, harsh and honest.

This dynamic has grown exponentially in a world increasingly defined by the Internet. There are now multiple ways in which people can receive accurate, no-holds-barred feedback from others on everything from their diet and hygiene habits to their performance on psychometric tests. The source of this feedback – a fair bit of it impersonal – has considerably less concern for emotion, utility, or viability of the information. This stands in contrast to, for example, the traditional methodology of feedback involving a superior writing a quarterly performance review.[26] Millennials/Zers have adapted to, and have benefitted from, an arena where feedback

" The gathering and use of information very quickly – the ability to assimilate a great deal of information, make sense of it, and act – are skills that are largely digital electronic. And the younger generations have that in spades. They are naturals at it."
– Senior military officer, Canadian Armed Forces

has become blunt, continuous, diverse, and available on demand. Employers must adjust their feedback approach to incorporate these elements to truly engage and embrace the Millennial mindset.

The culmination of these four factors – parents, peer/social, education, and technology – results in a simple conclusion: Millennials/Zers need feedback that is tailored to their mindset. They want feedback, and you, as an employer, must give it to them in a way that they will respond to. Without using strategies that target feedback to Millennials/Zers, businesses cannot hope to engage them and foster their talent. We now turn to some of these strategies.

Practical Advice for Giving Feedback to Millennials/Zers

The need for feedback seems to be embedded in the Millennial psyche. In contrast to previous generations, Millennials/Zers need a consistent and steady stream of feedback: "they ask for it and expect it … other generations have not felt they were as empowered to ask or sometimes demand the feedback."[27] Moderns assume that they were hired to do a job because, before being hired, they had already demonstrated the requisite skills and qualifications. As well, "people were so thankful just to have a job,"[28] and thus could not bring themselves to ask for anything more than the job itself. Millennials/Zers, as we have learned, have a very different outlook and are not afraid to make demands on their managers and workplace, especially regarding their need for feedback. In a recent EY (previously Ernst and Young) survey, 65 per cent of Millennial workers stated that being provided detailed guidance in daily work was moderately to extremely important; this is significant when compared to 39 per cent of Modern respondents. Furthermore, an overwhelming 85 per cent of Millennial workers agreed that their age-group peers wanted "frequent and candid performance feedback."[29]

> "My teammates and I expect feedback, good or bad, after every single shift on the ice. It is part of what gives us a strong support base and makes us feel comfortable taking risks in a high-speed game."
>
> – Conor Timmins, defenceman, Colorado Eagles professional minor league ice hockey team (age 21)

As both a manager and a professor, part of my job has been to give more feedback. An increasingly significant part of what I do in meetings, presentations, and customer calls is spend time thinking about feedback and how to give it. I do this actively, not passively as I did in the past. When I attend meetings, I must now actively listen to provide specific, in-depth feedback; this takes focus and additional time. A decade ago, I would spend perhaps 10 per cent of the time in a meeting thinking about feedback for my employees; today, it is more like 25 per cent to 30 per cent. Perhaps because of the time and effort required, experienced managers do not necessarily relish the idea of giving feedback. Indeed, in the past, before realizing the importance of feedback, I would give it as it occurred to me – and to be honest, often without sufficient thought – and primarily at the annual review, an often thoroughly unenjoyable hour.

However, business leaders must learn to appreciate the value of giving constant, consistent feedback despite the relative inefficacy of the annual or quarterly review. UCLA business professor Samuel Culbert has called, in a rather colourful way, for the end of the yearly review meetings. We may overstate his case, but not by much.[30] First, Culbert argues that the typical annual review is dishonest and fraudulent. Second, he has said that "they're just plain bad management." The problem with the practice, according to Culbert, is that periodic reviews create circumstances that help neither the employee nor the company to improve. As Culbert and his co-author, Larry Rout, argue, reviews do not promote candid discussions about workplace problems and their potential solutions.

Instead, when workers undergo a review, "they're going to talk about all their successes – it becomes total baloney."[31] Management participates in the charade: "the boss already has heard [from] his boss what they want to pay the [employee]. So, they come up with a review that's all backwards."[32] The process can frustrate employees, who may have a lot at stake from the quality of their review – from a raise or promotion to the determination of the general arc of their career. At the very least, employees want their contributions and talents to be recognized. Rather than using this ineffective method of giving feedback, Culbert suggests that management "just tell the employee what he or she needs to do to become more effective."[33]

The challenge of feedback begins within the organization. Firstly, Moderns need to challenge the belief, and their preconceptions, that giving feedback is an uncomfortable experience. Instead, they need to view the exercise as a means of improving the business. Secondly, Moderns need to be humble and realize that receiving feedback on one's feedback approach is a necessary part of the process. Moderns should ask their employees how they can improve in giving feedback and then learn, and apply, the requisite skills.[34] In addition, Moderns should embrace collaboration and engage in discussions with other managers on different techniques and their relative merits. Feedback, after all, is a multi-person activity. Finally, Moderns should embrace their role as managers; they are responsible, for better or worse, for the nurturing, motivation, and growth of Millennial employees. This process can be significantly simplified by giving feedback; a proactive attitude will turn feedback into a regular part of work life.

The Five Languages of Appreciation

One of the most down-to-earth and helpful approaches that Moderns should consider adding to their repertoire of feedback skills is outlined in Gary Chapman and Paul White's 2019 book *The 5 Languages of Appreciation in the Workplace: Empowering Organizations by Encouraging People*.[35] I really like this approach, to such a high degree that I have taught this method in new manager courses to hundreds of prospective managers.

Chapman and White applied the five languages, initially developed for use within families, to the workplace. They argue that there are five key ways to express appreciation for others, including subordinates and co-workers, in the workplace:

- words of affirmation;
- quality time;
- acts of service;
- tangible gifts;
- physical touch.

The concept of *affirmation* involves using words that let the person know that they have done something valuable. This is more involved than throwing out the occasional "good work!" – this will not suffice. For words of affirmation to be effective, it is essential they be specific. Praising a specific part of someone's performance makes the praise meaningful; this also shows that you were paying attention to what matters.

An example of this is saying that "I know that those figures were challenging and complex. You did a great job of making them understandable." Or "I really appreciate the extra effort you've been making to coach the new employee; her accuracy has improved dramatically with your help." To Millennials/Zers, the speed with which they receive feedback is essential. They would like to know your thoughts on their presentation immediately after they deliver it.

Quality time entails listening to the person rather than talking over them, thereby letting them express their ideas at length and in full. Simply having coffee with a person and giving them undivided, focused attention (something all too rare in this world) is a great way to reach those who desire and need quality time. For younger workers, time together with their colleagues, as a group, is valued because the desire is more to be part of a team.

Acts of service appeal to those who believe that talk is cheap and wonder why someone doesn't actually do something about it. For example, when my assistant is overloaded, I might perform an act of service and say to them, "Don't worry about it. I see you're swamped, so I'll do it myself." Physically taking on a task, and perhaps off-loading that work from someone else who might be overburdened, shows that you value that person and the work that they do. Another example is offering to help a colleague finish a project that is due the next day. The difference that I have seen among Millennials/Zers, though, is that they often want to work together with their colleagues rather than divide and conquer the work.

Closely related to acts of service is the giving of *tangible gifts*. The concept is not directly tied to the value of the present but more as an indication that the gift-giver thought of the person and bought something they knew would be appreciated. For example, it could be as simple as bringing your office-mate the new type of muffin from Tim Hortons, because you knew they wanted to try it. A typical tangible gift requested by Millennial employees is either time off after working long hours on a project, or a manager who is more flexible about their starting hour. Those that respond to tangible gifts are by no means materialistic: gifts need not cost a fortune. They just need to show appreciation (it's the thought that counts, as a Modern would say).

Finally, the fifth language of appreciation developed by Chapman and White is *physical touch*. In the family context, for which the authors were initially writing, this makes perfect sense. At work, however, one must take considerably more care applying this: its appropriateness is highly dependent on the setting, culture, and even genders involved. A high-five, a fist bump, or a two-handed handshake are all generally acceptable in the Western world. In some cultures – the French-Canadian culture of Montreal, for example – touch is more acceptable. In Montreal, men and women will often greet each other with a kiss on each cheek, something largely frowned upon and not usually done in Toronto. In the workplace, simply placing your hand on a shoulder, or a pat on the back, can resonate and indicate to the receiver that they are appreciated, or doing a good job.

This leads to the question of which language of appreciation should be used to provide optimal feedback.[36] The answer is that it is not easily determined. The proper response is often highly individual-specific and varies over time. I have taught this idea to well over a thousand people (mostly managers), and there is a fairly even spread of preference across the five languages. That said, we often tend to express ourselves in the language that we personally prefer, most likely because it's the one we're the best at giving – it just comes more naturally. The shortcoming is that if we wish to express appreciation to someone else, it is best done in the language to which they are most receptive, that they prefer. A good manager must, therefore, learn to speak all five languages to effectively express appreciation in the way that is best received by a diversity of subordinates.[37] And, of course, managers must be prepared to invest time to develop and apply the five languages of appreciation properly.

The Stop/Keep/Start Doing Approach

Applying his sks framework (stop/keep/start doing), Thomas DeLong of Harvard Business School identifies three questions one must ask for effective feedback:

• What should I stop doing?
• What should I keep doing?
• What should I start doing?[38]

Managers can use the sks framework both to provide effective feedback to Millennials/Zers and to ask these questions, in order to prompt meaningful conversations for upward feedback.

Alongside the use of the five languages of appreciation and the sks framework described above, I recommend the use of four other strategies:

• Balance the positive and negative feedback.
• Describe the problem.
• Involve the employee in the solution.
• Establish a follow-up expectation.[39]

The SMART Model

As a professor, I have experienced this Millennial/Gen Z need for feedback. For the last few years, I have found some of my students to be a bit irritating at times – they simply were demanding more feedback than, in previous years, I would have felt comfortable giving. Over time, the amount of feedback students expect has increased.

Those same Millennials/Zers, when they graduate from university, expect the same high level of feedback at their jobs. This is a fundamental shift – indeed, if I had to boil down the message of this chapter into one phrase, simply put, it would be: feedback was once top of mind for the manager; now it's at the top of the de facto job description of a manager.

Consultant Sema Burney, a former career adviser for MBA students at McGill, has shared a simple, explicit framework that my colleagues and I have been using to help managers give better feedback on an everyday basis (you may already be familiar with it in other contexts).[40] It is also a practical model that adapts well to giving feedback to Millennials/Zers.

Performance objectives are based on the following five criteria, captured in the acronym SMART (an apt reminder why it is important to set goals):

- specific;
- measurable;
- attainable;
- relevant;
- time-based.

Meeting these criteria is essential, not only so that employees get a real sense of the basis on which they are being evaluated but also so managers can streamline and standardize the feedback process.

The first aspect of the model is that the objectives must be *specific* to eliminate any ambiguity or misunderstanding. Objectives that are too general leave room for too much interpretation and can lead to a potential conflict between managers and employees. For example, suppose that a manager sets a performance goal to improve customer service. Being very general, it does not specify what aspect of customer service should be improved, nor how improvement will be evaluated – it could be based on customer feedback, observation, or any number of other metrics. An alternative, more specific objective could be to improve customer satisfaction by a certain percentage, based on survey results. In short, the less ambiguity, the less chance for misinterpretation from either side.

This leads to the importance of objectives being *measurable*. It is crucial to identify goals that are easily and accurately measured so that both manager and employee know the agreed-upon way to best achieve the objective and when it has been achieved. This is more straightforward when objectives can be quantified with hard numbers. For example, sales targets, market share, and financial data are usually easier to measure than intangible targets, such as being a strong team player or coaching another employee. Objectives dealing with soft skills are often the most difficult to evaluate. Nonetheless, with a little creativity, even intangible objectives can be written as SMART goals. For example, in order to encourage an employee to become more of a team player, it should be possible to formulate an objective based on the organization of a number of team events or participation in a certain number of cross-functional team projects.

The objectives must be *attainable*. Targets should be set to challenge the employee, but they must still be achievable, and something the employee wants to achieve. To that end, objectives should always be set collaboratively between managers and employees for the latter to feel ownership and take responsibility. This encourages employees to work hard toward their own, personalized goals, always with the assumption that they are realistic and realizable.

Objectives that are *relevant* are aligned with the overall strategic direction of the organization. Employees need to feel that their work is meaningful and contributes to the organization as a whole; consequently, objectives should be tied to broader departmental and organizational goals. Failure to do so can result in an employee becoming demotivated and confused about their role. In cases where the individual's objectives are misaligned with those of the broader organization, the employee may become frustrated working hard toward a goal perceived as having no value for the organization.

The final criterion of the SMART model is that objectives should be *time-based* or have a set time frame. Attaching a time constraint on the achievement of a goal can also be used to bring a sense of urgency to completion, thereby motivating employees and eliminating any misunderstanding regarding the relative importance of any given mandate.

Beyond feedback methods with individual employees, at a higher level, an organization should develop a broader system that utilizes different strategies to make the giving and receipt of feedback more efficient and uniform. This would also enable organizations to model their feedback processes directly on Millennial needs. By way of example, EY has created an online Feedback Zone where employees can request or submit feedback at any time. As well, each new hire is assigned a buddy for additional routine feedback.

Another example is found at Accenture, which offers ongoing training to hone their managers' critiquing skills. Feedback should not be confined to formal meetings.[41] It should be rapid and, if possible, instantaneous.

Millennials/Zers live in a world of instant gratification, where technology gives them the answers to their questions within seconds. Whenever they hear an interesting song, they immediately use an app to identify the artist and album before deciding whether to download it. When they post a status update on Facebook, they almost immediately receive feedback in the form of Likes, emoticons, and comments. Millennials/Zers do not wait, nor do they know how to. The world is moving so fast that there is risk in waiting. However, as detailed by Darrell Worthy, a professor of psychology at Texas A&M University who studied decision-making and motivation, this may not be entirely beneficial since "a lot of things that are valuable take time. But immediate gratification is the default response. It's difficult to overcome those urges and be patient and wait for things to come over time."[42] These behaviours, regardless of their beneficial or detrimental effects, transfer readily into the workplace. And perhaps above all else, they are responsible for the Millennial need for instantaneous, constant feedback.

For Millennials/Zers, feedback is a big part of what makes work exciting. Since halted or stifled growth is unacceptable in their eyes, it reassures them that they are still moving forward. If the key components of development and growth – including regular feedback, but also others that have been discussed throughout this book – are missing, Millennials/Zers do what they feel they must and search out other opportunities better oriented to their needs (young people are not afraid to quit their jobs).[43] Accommodating the Millennial need for feedback might actually lead to Millennial retention and talent development. Indeed, effective, tailored, and integrated feedback from the corporate to the individual levels just might enable Millennials/Zers to be more productive than ever before.

Finally, some advice for Millennials/Zers who may be reading this book. Many of you love feedback, but there are ways to more effectively seek feedback in your workplace. Feedback, like mentoring, is a two-way street that should be embraced by both sides. On that note, here are some tips from management coach Joel Garfinkle's book *Getting Ahead* on how Millennials/Zers could more effectively look for feedback:[44]

- *Schedule it.* Your colleague needs to be available. You'll need a private place, and plan ahead so the person has time to think.
- *Explain what you want.* Say, "I need your take on some of my recent decisions" or "How do I come across to our customers?"
- *Don't fish for compliments.* People will hold back if they doubt you want an honest assessment. Get right to the point and say, "I think I may be interrupting people or coming across as a jerk. How do you think I could improve my style?"
- *Ask for specifics.* It helps defuse the tension and makes feedback more honest and analytical. If they say you *always* do something, say, "Wow, I didn't realize I came off that way. I really don't want to give that impression. Can you think of a situation where I've done that recently?"
- *Don't be defensive.* This is the hardest part of receiving feedback, since it's so easy to blurt out questions like, "Why do you say that?" or "What does that mean?" Instead, take everything in with an open mind and reflect on your own behaviour. This leads into the next point.
- *Thank them.* Be appreciative. And ask for more feedback.
- *Approach others.* Ask the same questions and look for patterns in how feedback is requested and given.
- *Develop an action plan.* If you've done all of the above steps correctly, you should have some actionable material on how to improve and enhance your capabilities. After you've worked on your behaviour for at least a month or two, and you feel the urge to, make the rounds again.

As your generations increasingly become part of the managerial ranks, you too must learn to better provide feedback to fellow Millennials/Zers, and those who follow. As such, you will eventually need to learn how to give effective feedback. Consider your experience now, and how you approach it, as your training ground.

Millennials/Zers are the future of every organization. Moderns cannot ignore this; before they can expect anything from Millennials/Zers, Moderns must fulfil Millennials/Zers' expectations, especially when it comes to feedback. Feedback is their nourishment, so give it to them.

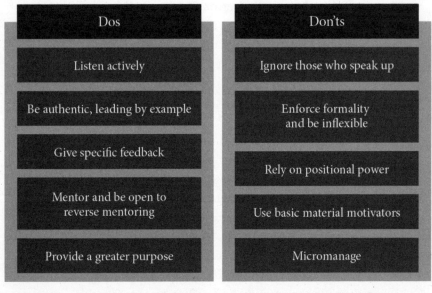

Figure 9.2
Quick checklist for leading Millennials/Zers

10

Similar but Different
Generation Zers Are Not Millennials

Millennials/Zers are now firmly established in the workplace, and the priority for managers should be to fully engage and integrate this growing population into their teams. That being said, there are some distinct differences between the Millennials and the generation beginning to enter the workforce – Generation Z[1] or the "iGeneration,"[2] which includes any person born between 1996 and 2010.[3] This generation is defined by a globalist mentality, digital nativity, and unprecedented levels of diversity. Generation Z's oldest constituents have already graduated from college and become part of the junior ranks of our workforce, and their presence will only become increasingly noticeable. I have a quite positive view of this generation; I am privileged to teach and travel with them, and I have eight or so work part-time for me most years. Not everyone shares my view. The wonderfully clever title of a 2019 article in *The Economist* called them "stressed, depressed and exam-obsessed."[4] As the average age of retirement continues to increase, the addition of this new population means that our modern workforce will now span *five* generations.[5] Managers will be challenged more than ever before when it comes to bringing out the most in their employees, regardless of the generation that formed them.

Given Gen Z's distinctive characteristics and growing presence in workplaces, I felt it important to have a chapter solely focused on this emerging generation, which, in its unique way, will now be the one challenging traditional ways of thinking, innovating, and changing the economy as we know it today. They too will be bringing their worldview to the workplace, a worldview that will evolve as they age, as it did with their older peers.[6]

The previous chapters presented a detailed analysis and set of recommendations for effectively managing Millennials/Zers. This chapter uses the same type of analysis, and ultimately presents a set of recommendations on how best to manage Generation Z as a bit different from Millennials. The subsequent sections are a little more condensed than the earlier ones, which blended Millennials and Zers. In part, this is because the research field surrounding the latter is still relatively nascent – namely in the case of research in the work setting. Nonetheless, the insights we can draw from available data, with the help of some informed inferences, are fascinating, indispensably valuable to understanding how managers can facilitate Generation Z's entrance into the workforce, and already relevant at this juncture in time.

Some may hold that Generation Z is far from having a significant presence in the workforce. But they will eventually, and I explain why managers need to keep this emerging cohort in the back (and sometimes even front) of their mind. Generation Z has many unique characteristics that both separate them from and connect them to Millennials in truly surprising ways.[7] Knowing those differentiating tendencies and perspectives is vital to understanding Generation Z's worldview. Once the Generation Z frame of mind and perspective is properly understood, the challenges of managing them can be addressed, thereby enabling your organization to benefit from the unique qualities and talents that generation brings to the workplace.

Why Worry about Gen Zers Now?

First and foremost, let's establish why this discussion is relevant at this point. While recent generations have varied in some incredible ways, there remain consistent patterns between generations that we can rely on. Namely, we can most likely accurately predict when each generation will peak in the workforce. In the case of the Millennial population, most estimates place that date around 2036.[8] As incredible as it may seem, we are closer to that date than we are to the turn of the last millennium.

In a world that changes as fast as ours has over the past twenty years, preparation and readiness are some of the most important qualities of a manager. Hence, it is essential for them to begin developing an awareness of the challenges, as well as the benefits, that the entrance of Generation Z into the workforce will present. The many firms that have struggled with the problem of Millennial retention (or ignored it to their disadvantage) can attest to the importance of this early preparation. This relevance is underscored by a recent study conducted by Deloitte that found that, in the United States, Gen Z constitutes more than one-quarter of the population, and is the most diverse generation in the nation's history.[9]

I suspect that, like generations before it, Millennial innovation will plateau when they, as a generation, reach the upper echelons within their organizations. This drop-off in innovation will force managers to look elsewhere for inspiration and for the spark of creativity that is needed to keep their business dynamic: they will have to be prepared to accept ideas and ways of thinking from the next generation of innovators, the Gen Zers.

This connects with the school of emergent strategy. As mentioned earlier in this book, there are two great schools of strategic thought: one from Harvard's Michael Porter, the other from McGill's Henry Mintzberg.[10] As a reminder, you can contrast their two views as follows: Porter's takes a more deliberate approach to strategy, while Mintzberg's emphasizes emergent strategy. Both are still taught; I teach Porter's Generic Strategies and his Five Forces model in an undergraduate strategy course at McGill. But which is most useful today? Let's briefly explore both approaches.

The world of *deliberate strategy* is one that I remember well from my days as a corporate manager at IBM and then as an executive teacher at Oxford University and the London Business School. It was strategy planning weekends at posh hotels in the English countryside, where we sat in rooms discussing the Five Forces in our particular industry and what we would change in the model if we had a fairy's magic wand (I'd like to thank my old Oxford colleague David Feeney – I learned that from him).

This worked well in its day, back in the 1980s and early '90s – wonderful times now that I look back on them – when the past was quite helpful in predicting the future. However, the nature of the world today no longer lends itself, by and large, to this type of strategy.

Emergent strategy is the view that strategy emerges over time as intentions collide with and accommodate a changing reality. It is a set of actions or behaviour, consistent over time, "a realized pattern [that] was not expressly intended"[11] in the original planning of strategy. Emergent strategy implies that an organization is learning what works in practice. Given today's world, I think the use of emergent strategy by managers is on the upswing, and here is why.

The relatively stable world of my corporate career (or at least part of it) is now mostly extinct. At times, it seems the world has gone nuts. Let me count some ways: COVID-19, the rise of China as a potential superpower, the pulling back of United States with regard to international affairs, the reality of climate change and its causes, the continued growth of the international class of people known as the super-rich. As one writer put it in the *New York Times*, "For a moment, all the swans seemed black," and that was before the Coronavirus crisis hit the world.[12]

Strategy has shifted in the last decade to a point where the planning school no longer has the street cred it once had. It is precisely because we cannot, try as we may, control the variables that factor into business decisions that Mintzberg's emergent strategy is so useful.

Porter's ideas are still relevant. My colleagues and I still teach them, so I still believe in them, and when I talk to corporate CEOs, they say they still use them as part of their thinking on strategic planning. But they are getting to be a bit old school in today's world. Mintzberg's emergent strategy ideas simply seem more relevant to the world we live in today – they reflect the fact that our plans will fail, and we must always be prepared to pivot. This is not to say that planning isn't useful, but other than some long-term technology plans, the days of the five-year and even two-year plans are gone. Emergent strategy is the order of the day in most companies that I work with. You must be much more fleet of foot, and strategic flexibility is what we are looking for in most industries. The boundaries are more fluid now. For many, albeit not all, even knowing what industry you are in is not as clear-cut as it once was. This makes industry analysis more difficult. Value chains are now shared across firm boundaries and, at times, even with competitors.

This leads us to see the value of boundary spanners in emergent strategy. *Boundary spanners* are people who have one foot in the organization and one foot in the turbulent outside world. In a world of turbulence and disruptive innovation, their role is even more important. They help strategy makers, typically those in the C-suite, to develop better strategy more aligned with what is happening outside the organization, thus allowing organizations to be better aligned with the outside world.

Which brings us to Generation Z. Newer, and typically younger, members of our organizations are the ones who are more apt to be boundary spanners. Therefore, in most organizations, it is critically important to spend more time listening to them to get their input to develop a better emergent strategy. Earlier, I came to this same conclusion regarding Millennials/Zers as crucial for organizations that wish to innovate and remain relevant. When looking at Generation Z more specifically, the relevance of this point increases tenfold. Listening to your younger employees is not only important but also necessary if you want successful strategies designed for today's, not yesterday's, world. The good news for those in the C-suite is that you still get to decide!

Members of Generation Z, much like their Millennial predecessors, will not be shy about sharing their thoughts and ideas about the direction that your team could and should take. Their enthusiasm and creativity should be channelled in the same way that you currently channel the Millennials' enthusiasm. Unlike their Millennial counterparts, however, Generation Z prefer face-to-face interaction and communication (though this evolved a bit during the work-from-home of the COVID world) and, hence, will be much more comfortable sharing their perspective during team meetings than over e-mail, as Millennials are wont to do.[13]

Similarly, the global mindset of Generation Z will be much more pronounced than that of the Millennials. Managers will have to (and morally should) build and prepare a more diverse, inclusive, and open workspace.[14] Collectively, Generation Z will also have their own human capital – including the technological aptitude needed to not only survive but also drive progress in the workplace. Technological baseline skills that may have taken earlier generations time to get accustomed to will be innate to Generation Z.[15] While Millennials became familiar with technological devices at a relatively young age, Generation Z cannot remember the pre-iPhone world and can use technology in a manner that is significantly more integrative than previous generations ever did. When I get on the elevator at McGill's Business School, I am amused to see how often undergraduate students are on their smartphones. Increasingly, that is also true of my morning ride on the Montreal Metro.

Ultimately, much as it is up to Generation X to find value in their Millennial successors, it will be up to Millennials to identify value in their successors and to integrate them into the workforce in a way that only they know how. While managers from previous generations can help ease this process of integration, the familiarity that adjacent generations share, and the bonds that this familiarity creates, is what will enable new entrants into the workforce to more quickly feel genuinely accepted.[16]

The "I" Generation's Worldview

Generation Z is tech innate (the first, but not the last, generation to achieve this), has a realist mentality, and displays a preference toward globalism that is greater than any of its predecessors. While Gen Z is far from a carbon copy of the Millennial generation, understanding the paradigm shifts that occurred as a result of Millennials (or on their watch) is essential to understanding Gen Z's worldview.[17] For example, while Millennials witnessed the birth of the current technological revolution and the creation of the Internet, Gen Z doesn't remember a world without Facebook, Amazon, Netflix, and Google (referred to collectively by the acronym FANG).[18] Similarly, while Millennials helped elect a Black president and legalize gay marriage, Gen Z assumes these things as just a part of everyday life. The social progressiveness spearheaded by Millennials caused their successor generation to be by nature globalist and encouraging of diversity.

While you may see yourself as having had an incredibly different upbringing from your Millennial counterparts or employees, try to imagine that Generation Z does not remember a world before 9/11 or the Columbine High School shootings. The watershed events that fundamentally altered our modern reality are simply not a part of everyday discourse for this generation. Much as some readers grew up in a post-Watergate era, which caused politicians to be viewed with a certain skepticism that would have been hard for their parents to fully comprehend, Gen Z's conceptualization of the world might be hard to grasp at first. Understanding the root causes of these differences in perception will help managers better account for them when interacting with their Generation Z employees.

A helpful example to understand these differences comes in the form of financial markets. Think of the vastly different state of markets between when the Millennial generation was growing up and when Generation Z was. While

Millennials were brought up in a time of economic prosperity and were surprised to find an uninviting job market when they emerged into the workforce, Generation Z came of age during the recession, which has moulded their perception of the workforce as an uber-competitive and unwelcoming environment.[19]

The Challenges of Managing Generation Z

As managers prepare for the ongoing introduction of more and more Generation Z members to their teams, they must understand how to nurture and encourage the capabilities and talents of this generation. By now, managers should be aware that younger generations (namely through the example of Millennials) have a different relationship to authority and respond differently than previous generations to traditional management methods.[20] While it was previously possible to get the best out of team members by moulding them into the perfect company member, younger generations react much more positively to encouraging guidance rather than outright orders. And this will be especially true of Generation Z. Rather than attempting to bend employees to their will, managers should focus on guiding and encouraging their young employees.[21]

Distinctive Characteristics of Gen Z

To facilitate the process of Generation Z entering the workforce, managers should understand the five major characteristics of this cohort:

- commitment to equality, diversity, and inclusion;
- digital savviness;
- importance of job security;
- competitiveness;
- comfort with exchanging and co-creating ideas.

The first and foremost major characteristic of Generation Z is its unwavering *commitment to equality, diversity, and inclusion in the workspace* – a product of their highly progressive early environment.[22] While the moral argument was always there for companies to promote and actively build diverse and inclusive work environments, this will not be optional if they wish to attract and retain Gen Z workers. It is simple: Gen Z grew up in a world that strove to advance by leaps and bounds in terms of social and economic equality.[23] These ideals characterize their political and economic beliefs, with many Gen Zers fiercely supporting national political figures such as Bernie Sanders.

They will take a different tack and refuse to stand for the previously accepted status quo. Generation Z will expect the same out of their environment and, therefore, workplace. This not only is the case for Gen Z but also will very likely be a trend that grows in importance for the subsequent generation. If a company does not have an evidently inclusive workspace, it will be actively turning away Gen Z talent. Passing up a fraction of your potential employees can lead to several adverse outcomes. For every inept employee who scrolls past your job posting, an adept one does as well.

Diversity will most importantly mean gender and racial, but it is progressing beyond these to include diversity in areas that we cannot see with our eyes, such as social class. One example is introverts/ambiverts/extroverts,[24] which is an area of research that I have been exploring, inspired by someone who has become a colleague, Susan Cain, and her book *Quiet*. Though I have interviewed over 500 C-suite executives about being an introvert/extrovert and where they fall on that spectrum, it is not something that you can know (at least generally) by just a glance – it can only come from getting to know them. Additionally, managers need to apply diversity to the work life of this generation as well. Meaningful, varied experiences and assignments are going to keep young workers engaged. A more nuanced realization of diversity is part of what this generation is looking for.

The second major trait is their *digital savviness*. Managers need to nurture this aptitude since it will only become more important as the world pushes toward cloud computing, AI, and virtual co-creation.[25] As mentioned earlier, Gen Z has no memory of a world that wasn't connected. Taking a page from how managers have to leverage diversity to create meaning for the Gen Z workforce, managers can apply the same strategy in reverse and leverage Gen Z's technological aptitude.[26] For example, let's say new software or technology must be used for an upcoming project. No one in the firm is familiar with the technology or has used anything similar in the past. A manager can give the task to the employee they have known awhile and who delivers reliable results. Or they can give the assignment to the untested, unknown, recent university graduate. The answer seems obvious, right? Give it to your employee who is reliable and has been with the company for a while. After all, you know you will get a good return; nothing is more reliable at predicting the future than past experiences. While this might seem obvious, I would argue that the dilemma is a little trickier. While it is true that the tempting short-term solution would be to assign the proven employee to the project, here is a real opportunity for a manager if they just put some trust in their younger subordinate. Giving the assignment to the younger employee will not only provide real meaning to their work but also potentially yield a better result, as the younger employee is better able to adapt to this new technology. So, trust younger employees a little more when it comes to technology-heavy assignments, or make it a collaborative effort between your proven employees and younger, more digitally adept, talents. A big takeaway: there is tremendous value in the overexposure to technology that Generation Z has experienced.

The third characteristic of this incoming generation as it pursues employment is *job security* – Gen Z wants flexibility, culture, and career growth.[27] Unlike Millennials, who see themselves as fundamentally entrepreneurial, Gen Z, though many also wish to be entrepreneurs, is more likely to seek a career at an established international firm – likely a result of growing up in a post-2008-recession world. As previously discussed, the stable and prosperous upbringing that Millennials experienced clashed with the economic reality they met after college graduation. The 2008 financial crash changed job market expectations for Millennials, at the time they were least expecting it. Conversely, Generation Z was coming of age during these troubling economic times. They watched older siblings struggle to find jobs once they graduated from college, an idea that immediately shaped their understanding of what they could and should expect out of the job market. In short: they understood that there would be no free meal for them. This mindset of scarcity largely influences Gen Z to value job security over other factors, though things may well evolve.[28]

This pursuit of job security and a mindset of scarcity relates to Generation Z's fourth major characteristic: *competitiveness*. From grades to starting salaries to those who had the most fun last weekend, members of Gen Z are massively competitive in their quest to lead a "fulfilling life."[29] While they will be all in favour of collaboration and co-creation with their co-workers, their fear of failure will push them to sometimes be overly competitive with those that surround them. Interestingly, for example, Gen Z places competitive pay over any other benefit a job may offer. This shows that it still lacks a holistic understanding of what a positive and engaging workplace can provide as well as create. Thus, it will be important for managers to show these younger employees how a well-rounded, high-performing team can deliver results that are far superior to those any single individual can deliver, no matter how significant this individual's merit or accomplishments might be.

Lastly, and potentially a little surprising considering their competitive streak, is Generation Z's *comfort with exchanging and co-creating ideas*.[30] Generation Z is far more comfortable with the exchange of ideas than generations of the past.[31] With less exposure to the traditional professor-student dynamics in their university classrooms and instead encouraged to participate in small-group discussions, Gen Z's understanding of the flow of information and the creation of ideas is a little different from previous generations. They will speak up at your staff meetings – not to show off or because they think this is how they will get a raise, but because they genuinely believe their interaction will advance the conversation. And if managers are doing their jobs, most of the time, it will! This is an inherent part of Gen Z's human capabilities, and managers should understand this unique knowledge base and form of knowledge creation as an asset that gives this young generation an edge in tomorrow's workforce. Increasingly, and for the reasons mentioned in the preceding competitiveness section, it will be useful for managers to encourage this peer-to-peer mentality, both in their Generation Z employees and beyond.

Related to this last trait, Generation Z is also characterized by open communication, even in the face of uncomfortable issues. It's not uncommon to find Generation Z openly engaging in conversation amongst one another about stigmatized topics, like mental health. However, this kind of discourse is not as prominent in the workplace. In fact, in a 2021 report published by Deloitte, researchers uncovered that "although nearly half of millennials and Gen Zs (48%) report feeling more stressed since the start of the COVID-19 pandemic, their employers most likely don't know how much they've been affected."[32] When it comes to managing this generation, we shouldn't overlook the struggles they've faced in light of the pandemic, especially when it comes to completing their education and entering the workforce in such an uncertain time. As such, support is key – Gen Zers will be open to talking to you, but only if the door is open for the discussion.

Take, for example, the issue of salary. "Talking about pay can be uncomfortable," writes Chloe Berger, a columnist for *Fortune* magazine, in March 2022, "but Gen Z and millennial workers are no longer afraid to have awkward conversations if that means getting paid what they're worth."[33] Gen Z are using social media platforms like TikTok to talk about their pay with strangers. If not addressed in the office, this generation is taking the opportunity to discuss their salaries online in order to secure jobs with higher pay, more benefits, and greater purpose.

These are today's five traits. As our world changes, they will undoubtedly morph in new directions to some degree, but understanding these five is an excellent starting place.

Responding to the Great Resignation

The preceding considerations bring into question a larger phenomenon that was observed during the COVID-19 pandemic: the Great Resignation. Unknowingly coined by Anthony Klotz, an associate professor of management at Texas A&M University, the Great Resignation refers to the mass exodus and job hopping of employees during the pandemic. According to an April 2022 article published in the *Financial Times*, official American workforce data showed that 4 million workers had quit in April 2021, about 2.7 per cent of the entire workforce and the highest level on record.[34] Within this unprecedented shift, Gen Zers had pivoted careers the most of any group during the pandemic, with a 59.6 per cent increase in job hopping, according to the earlier mentioned *Fortune* article.[35]

The question becomes: how can managers ensure that Gen Zers don't abandon their current jobs in search of other opportunities? At the core of this issue is communication: talk to your Gen Z employees about what drives them. What kinds of diversity initiatives and metrics do Gen Zers want to see more of? What kind of security are you offering your employees to ensure their financial safety and stability? And most importantly, are your Gen Zers finding purpose in their work? Talking to a Gen Zer about these issues may seem daunting, but an open line of communication can help you to carefully curate and nurture an environment in which they feel valued and heard – which was a driving force for the Great Resignation. Consider alternative modes of listening and mentoring, and don't be afraid to get uncomfortable.

Despite the work sphere traditionally being subordinate-superior, managers can adopt and encourage reverse mentorship with Generation Z employees, a topic covered in detail in chapter 9. As a reminder, traditional mentorship is when a manager or more experienced co-worker teaches a new employee a skill to successfully accomplish their job. Reverse mentoring is simply the encouragement of younger employees to share their specific skill set with their managers and co-workers when appropriate. It can be something as simple as manipulating a time and expense app or learning some time-saving software tricks. Managers should understand that mentoring and knowledge aren't exclusive to experience, and that younger generations as well have skills that can be taught.[36]

Managers should also take note: like Millennials, Gen Zers value feedback. In fact, even more. As much as Millennials love feedback, Zers are digital natives that know little but digital worlds full of real-time feedback (likes, shares, comments, etc.), so it makes them even more desirous of feedback than their Millennial cousins.[37] However, while Millennials prefer digital feedback, Gen Zers will prefer feedback through face-to-face conversations.[38] And they want it often: 60 per cent of Gen Zers want multiple check-ins from their manager during the week; of those, 40 per cent want the interaction with their boss to be daily or several times a day.[39]

While the current workforce is still taking shape, it is worth noting that Generation Z's early career experience is vastly different from that of generations past. With the COVID-19 pandemic shifting everything into the virtual world, Gen Z has entered the workforce virtually. Many of them have never worked in an office – their experiences as post-grads are primarily through virtual meetings and online coffee chats.

According to a 2021 *Forbes* article, lower productivity and increased boredom are key issues faced by Gen Zers through remote work. According to a 2021 study published by Ten Spot, a workforce engagement platform headquartered in New York, 54 per cent of Gen Zers report being less productive when working from home. In order to help Gen Zers succeed in their efforts from home, Ten Spot's co-founder and chief brand officer Sammy Courtright suggests that managers offer increased support to these entry-level employees by conducting more frequent check-ins and ensuring that they have the proper tools to work constructively from home. Boredom also creates a barrier to work for Gen Zers. According to the study, 48 per cent confess that they're bored working from home. In this case, it's important for more senior managers to find ways to connect with these employees, either by creating opportunities for social engagement or by helping the Gen Zers find their own purpose within the company.

While Gen Zers have become accustomed to working remotely – say, from their couches – there is a palpable feeling of wanting to return to the office, at least for a few days a week. According to an August 2021 article published in *Time* magazine, Gen Zers are itching for in-person interactions, support, and feedback, all of which will contribute to their overall productivity and sense of purpose in their work.[40] With COVID-19 restrictions easing and stress levels lowering, Gen Zers are among the first in line to set up a desk in an office and to experience the joys of conversations by water coolers. As managers, it is important to recognize this desire and support Gen Zers in their transition. For most of these employees, all they have ever known is the virtual work environment. As you bring employees back into the office, make sure to be patient with them. Actively listen to their concerns and try to adapt your management style in order to support their new and changing needs.

Meeting Challenges with Proactive Preparation

As stated at the outset of this chapter, there is still a little bit of time before Generation Z becomes a driver in the current workforce, and their full participation will not happen overnight. However, beginning the process of preparing your team and organization for this new generation will ensure that their entrance does not blindside you. Too often, managers have been reactionary in their inclusion of younger generations to their teams and, as a result, have suffered retention and engagement problems. Gen Z provides managers with a chance to avoid the same mistake.

A key to achieving this early preparation comes in building a solid understanding of the major qualities of Generation Z, discussed above. These characteristics help us define Gen Z and provide a path to understanding their social framework. From here, we can infer effective ways to manage them. A few examples of what implementing these ideas into management of Gen Zers would look like:

- sharing personal experience when hiring;
- leveraging this generation's technological skills;
- providing opportunities to showcase their technological aptitude;
- incentivizing initiative and intrapreneurship;
- surrounding them with diverse employees and projects;
- treating each Gen Z employee more as a personal contact than as a subordinate.

Understandably, as the Generation Zers mature and join the workforce, it will become increasingly more critical for managers to understand them. Hopefully, this chapter has kick-started reflection on how to welcome and effectively integrate this new generation into your teams, providing a jumping-off point for managers to explore how best to deal with it. The future is exciting with information and research to come as Generation Z becomes more established in the workplace. With time, more informed recommendations can be made, and hopefully, the workplace will become a happier, healthier, and more productive environment for all.

11

Managing Upward and Being Managed by Millennials/Gen Zers
Key to Being a Really Useful Manager

This chapter is first and foremost written for members of the younger generations wanting to manage upward, mainly in the context of Generation Xers and boomers. We have also included advice for those of an older generation on how to allow yourself to be managed by someone younger, and how to train them to work more effectively with you. I realize that for some boomers/Xers, their manager is younger than they are – whether it be an Xer or, increasingly, a Millennial/Zer – but, for the sake of clarity and simplicity, I am going to assume that your manager is older than you are. If, on the other hand, your manager is of your generation, I assume that you understand them better than a member of a different generation would. But, based on my experience and hundreds of conversations with C-suite members, the same principles broadly apply.

The most important part of being a great manager is focusing on the people who work for you. Perhaps the second most important – and this is especially true when working with Millennials and Generation Zers – is learning to effectively manage upward. Doing this well can be a great help to the people who work for you, not only for them to feel valued and heard but also to create a more dynamic and creative work setting. This is because the people you work for can provide resources, promotions, direction, and help to you and your people, helping all to prosper in the organizational world. Leadership has evolved from being mainly about authority to being about influence, so learning to appreciate and adapt to people with different perspectives, priorities, and personalities is a key skill to develop. Managing up allows you to practise navigating and influencing people who approach work differently than you do. Learn how to look beyond your own needs and perspectives and consider the needs and perspectives of others. This will help you to manage upward and also manage your people and your peers: great skills to learn early in your career.

We all have bosses. The CEO reports to the board of directors, who in turn work for the best interests of the shareholders and stakeholders, both large and small. Almost all of us work for somebody. When you speak with entrepreneurs, they talk about the incredible power of customers, their business angels, spouses, and suppliers. Liz Simpson in a Harvard Business School Management Update offers this insight: "The goal of managing upward up is not to curry favour ... it's more effective."[1] It is not about kissing upward, but rather, as the 2014 HBR 20-Minute Manager Series put it, "the aim is to have a mutually beneficial relationship."[2]

To my mind, there are four key principles to successfully managing upward:

- understand your boss's communication style;
- understand what motivates your boss;
- along with problems, bring solutions;
- no surprises.

The first, and arguably most important, principle is to *understand your boss's communication style*.[3] Are they a reader or a listener? Do they like e-mails, Zoom calls, meetings over the phone, or in-person exchanges? Meetings set up using online calendars or brief discussions as you pass in the hallway? Do they prefer early meetings, lunch meetings, or meetings over coffee at the local café? As mentioned earlier, over the last five years I have been studying quiet or introverted leaders in conjunction with Susan Cain's Quiet Leadership Institute. If your boss is more of an introvert, they are more likely, according to my research, to be a reader, to appreciate receiving material ahead of time, and to favour meetings set up ahead of time. All of this because they much prefer taking their time to do their research, analyze the information, and think it through rather than giving spontaneous comments. Extroverts tend to like to talk things through – often off-the-cuff – in-person, and frequently while running into colleagues in the hallway.

Each of us tends to prefer to communicate in a certain way. While this may seem an obvious statement, it is often something that many of us fail to acknowledge. We like to think that, as competent managers or employees, we can get our point across to all our team members, regardless of our or their communication preferences. While this may be the case, being cognizant of the fact that we – as well as the people around us – do have communication preferences can impact our responses, for better or worse. It is about becoming aware of how your boss likes to be communicated with, and integrating that awareness into your communication style. Use your strengths, absolutely, but learn to be flexible and lean into your interlocutor's preferred style.

For the Xers and boomers reading this section, we should let our people know how we like to be communicated with, making it clear and easy to grasp, and provide younger people with an explanation of why we like that approach. As discussed in an earlier chapter, the Millennials and Gen Xers are generations for whom never apologizing and never explaining are bad ideas.[4] When we explain our decisions and perspectives, it gives younger people the chance to improve on our ideas, and to keep us more in touch with today's world.

Tangentially, we have to understand both how our people like to be communicated with and how we like to be communicated with. Clearly, this is quite a modern notion. Some twenty-five years ago, the whole office would have had to adapt to the communication style of the boss, but today we need to go out of our way to find out each person's preferred way of being communicated with and, to a considerable degree, lean into that. The HBR 20-Minute Manager Series advises that "it is also important to clarify your own work style with your manager in the interest of practicality and transparency."[5] Today, more than ever, it is a two-way street, though as the series pointed out, you are still the boss. Just don't overdo it.

The second principle is to *understand what motivates your boss*.[6] Another helpful way to think about this could be: what is their agenda? When I teach new managers, I am always surprised by how many people don't know what their boss's top five priorities are for the year. This is not a new phenomenon. In a classic 2005 *Harvard Business Review* article, Harvard's John Gabarro and John Kotter say, "some superiors spell out their expectations very explicitly. But most do not. Ultimately, the burden falls on the subordinate to find out what the boss's expectations are."[7] If you can help your boss achieve one of their top five priorities, they will like you very much and consider you a star employee. What are they focused on this year? The answer to this question and follow-up questions to discover why these priorities are important to them will enable you to be more creative in coming up with ways to go forward. Don't wait for them to tell you their priorities – take them for a coffee and ask them. This will in turn help you guide your people in how the organization as a whole can better accomplish its goals.

In most organizations, the strategy or central direction comes from the top, the C-suite and the CEO in particular. In a world of more emergent strategy, this often develops at the bottom of the organizational pyramid, but is still given more solid direction when it reaches the top of the pyramid. Choices are made and they must be well communicated to the rest of the organization. The other C-suite executives and their goals must, or least should, dovetail with the CEO's overall direction, which cascades down to the front-line people. Like a rowing team, by all rowing in unison, we can make more progress, rather than going in several directions at once; a rather ineffective way of moving forward. Thus, from the top down, a manager's annual four or five priorities should contribute to their manager's four or five top items and so on through the organization, ultimately giving every employee clarity and focus to deliver their part to the overall strategy.

Managers need to make clear not only what motivates them but also why those particular priorities, and then communicate this reasoning clearly and frequently to Millennials and Gen Zers. Beyond frequent explanations of the whys, adopt a great willingness to be reverse-mentored by your younger employees and, based on input from your people, fine-tune – and sometimes even radically change – strategies.

The third principle is simple and concise: *along with problems, bring solutions.* When I became a manager at IBM back in the 1980s, I was taught that you never approached your manager with a problem without also presenting a solution. Now, in all honesty, some of my early efforts were pretty unimpressive, and I am sure John Holden and Bill Soden, my early bosses, must have chuckled after I left their offices. But they were teaching me something: they were training me. Over time, I would bother them less and less as I came up with my own solutions, working with my own team. When I did come to them, they knew that it was important, and that I really wanted and needed their wisdom and support. Never go to your boss without some ideas on how to solve the problem at hand. Don't forget to enlist the advice of your own people to come up with solutions before you go to your manager. Much like me, you won't immediately come up with final solutions, but you will progressively get more skilled, all the while creating goodwill with your manager by showing a willingness to problem solve. Jeffrey Pfeffer, a professor of organizational behaviour at Stanford and author of *Power: Why Some People Have It and Others Don't*, agrees with this view and said in a 2014 *Harvard Business Review* article, "Problems don't make people happy and bringing unsolved problems to your manager makes you look like you are not doing your job."[8] There can be limits to this, though, as Harvard Business School professor Linda Hill said in the same article, "Some people, afraid of not having the right solution in hand, don't do anything. If there is a problem and you don't have a solution, don't just sit around doing nothing, go ask your boss for help."

The last principle is a biggie: *no surprises*. Keep your manager in the know so they appear competent and in charge to their manager. I never, ever want the principal of our university to say to my dean, "Karl is doing [fill in the blank]. Did you know about it?" and the dean to have to say, "No." I have made a conscious effort to let every dean I have worked with know anything that might get on the radar of the principal, so that they appear fully in charge of their part of the university. But in today's world, this relationship goes both ways. Try very hard not to surprise your people with major direction changes. As I said earlier: make them part of the process. Not only is that great leadership in today's world but it also makes for better strategy.

Acknowledgments

First, I thank my family, Brigitte and our two wonderful children, Erik and Marie-Eve, for their support during the lengthy process of writing this book. I also thank some of my colleagues around the world for their encouragement and intellectual inspiration, particularly, Henry Mintzberg, Phillip Levy, Saku Mantere and others at McGill; Julian Birkinshaw at LBS; Richard Whittington at Oxford; Amy Edmondson at HBS; my former doctoral student and now colleague and friend, Nicolay Worren, at the Norwegian University of Life Sciences; and Quy Huy of INSEAD. Also, I thank the many Millennial/Generation Z students at McGill and Oxford I had the pleasure of teaching and spending time with, as research assistants on our annual Hot Cities of the World; over the last eleven years I have travelled with thirty undergrads to Israel, the UAE, India, South Africa, Russia, Mongolia/South Korea, Doha/ Hong Kong/Jakarta/Bali, Chile/Colombia, and, in 2019, Tokyo, Bangkok, and Hong Kong. The undergrads and MBA candidates who deserve special mention include: Avneet Bhabra, Tegan Boaler, Lainie Yallen, Aya Schechner, Dan Schechner, Liam Timmins, Margaret Snell, Rafi Azari, Dr Mali Worme, Dr Anais Hausvater, Dr Avigyle Grunbaum, Marie-Claire Laflamme-Sanders, Ishana Gopaul, Sienna Zampino, Judith Lawrence, Aly Haji, Mike Ross, Audreann Cote Fournier, Lauren Kirigin, Arjun Kapur, Matthieu Manzoni, and Eytan Bensoussan. I must highlight the outstanding work of editing, fact-checking, and formatting (not to mention some welcome additions to my text) by Mo Rubineau, Eleanor Gasparik, and Didier Giovannangeli, and on the publishing side McGill-Queen's University Press managing editor Kathleen Fraser and finally publisher Philip Cercone, all of whom considerably improved this book!

I would also like to thank the many leaders who were interviewed for this book including *Quiet* author Susan Cain; F1 driver Lewis Hamilton; hockey great Ken Dryden; skier Jennifer Heil; three-time Olympic gold medal winner Kim St Pierre; former chairman of the Joint Chiefs of Staff General Martin Dempsey; head of the Canadian Military General Wayne Eyre; former prime ministers Paul Martin, Brian Mulroney, Stephen Harper, and Joe Clark, and current prime minister Justin Trudeau; Nobel Prize winner Muhammad Yunus; and Sir Richard Branson. Plus, close to a thousand CEOs thanks to the CEO *Series*, a weekly radio show heard on Bell Media radio stations across Canada, that is in its tenth year; the CEO Insights course that McGill University has allowed me to run for the MBA program for over a dozen years; co-authoring a biweekly column, Indigenous Leaders, for the *Globe and Mail*, Canada's national newspaper; and doing a weekly video interview for the *Globe and Mail* of CEOs and leading business school professors for nine years. This wonderful access to some of the world's top leaders has given me a view from boomers, Xers, and older Millennials. As a professor who largely teaches undergrads, I have been blessed to be reverse-mentored by over 4,000-plus undergrads and 1,000-plus MBAs at McGill and many during my five years teaching at Oxford.

Key Postmodern Terms

Agent or agency Someone assumed to have authority and power; causal force.

Chronophonism The Modern attitude that time is chronological or linear. Postmodernists are opposed to chronophonism.

De-centring Absence of anything at the centre or any overriding truth. This means concentrating attention on the margins.

Deconstruction A Postmodern method of analysis. Its goal is to undo all constructions. Deconstruction tears a text apart, and reveals its contradictions and assumptions; however, its intent is not to improve, revise, or offer a better version of the text.

Differed Difference in the sense of dispute, conflict, or disagreement about the meaning of language.

Difference A structuring principle that suggests definition rests not on the entity itself but in its positive and negative references to other texts. Meaning changes over time, and ultimately the attribution of meaning is put off, postponed, or deferred forever.

Discourse All that is written and spoken and all that invites dialogue or conversation.

Heroic Modern social scientists sometimes focus on one event or person. In so doing, Postmodernists argue, they create heroes and attach excessive importance to the capacities of a single individual to effect change or influence specific, dramatic events. Postmodernists, rejecting this approach (heroic analysis), neither focus on individuals nor construct heroes. Many Postmodernists call for the end of the subject, the death of the author.

Hyper-reality Reality has collapsed, and today it is exclusively image, illusion, or simulation. The model is more real than the reality it supposedly represents. The hyper-real is "that which is already reproduced."[1] It is a model "of a real without origin or reality."[2]

Hyper-space Postmodern term referring to the fact that our modern concepts of space are meaningless. Space doesn't act according to modern assumptions. It has been annihilated, and spatial barriers have disappeared. Everything is in geographical flux, constantly and unpredictably shifting in space.

Imploding, implosion Tendency for phenomena in a Postmodern world to explode inwardly, thus destroying themselves and one's assumptions about them.[3] Meaning disappears altogether.[4]

Intertextual Infinitely complex interwoven interrelationships, "an endless conversation between the texts with no prospect of ever arriving at or being halted at an agreed point."[5] Absolute intertextuality assumes that everything is related to everything else.

Logocentric An adjective used to describe systems of thought that claim legitimacy by reference to external, universally truthful propositions. Postmodernists are opposed to logocentric thought. They say such systems are really grounded in self-constituted logic. They consider them circular, self-referential, and self-satisfying. As Postmodernists see it, no grounds exist for defensible external validation or substantiation.[6]

Narrative Postmodern opinion of this concept varies, depending on the type of narrative under discussion. Postmodernists severely criticize meta-narratives, global worldviews, and master codes. Meta-narratives are modern and assume the validity of their own truth claims; however, mini-narratives, micro-narratives, local narratives, and traditional narratives are just stories that make no truth claims and are, therefore, more acceptable to Postmodernists.

Pastiche A free-floating, crazy-quilt, collage, hodgepodge patchwork of ideas or views. It includes elements of opposites such as old and new. It denies regularity, logic, or symmetry; it glories in contradiction and confusion.

Privilege To give special attention or attribute priority to an argument, a person, an event, or a text. Postmodernists oppose privileging any specific perspective.

Le quotidien Daily life analysis or everyday life focus. Postmodernists see it as a positive alternative to global theory.

Reader Observer. Postmodernism is reader-oriented and gives readers the power of interpreting a text that, in modern terms, belonged to the author. Postmodern readers are dramatically empowered.

Reading Understanding, interpretation. One speaks in terms of "my reading," "your reading," or "a reading," without reflecting on the adequacy, the validity of said reading.

Rhetoric In the modern sense denotes "artificial eloquence" as opposed to serious, rigorous, scientific discourse. But for Postmodernists it is taken in its more classical definition to mean oratory, the artful presentation of ideas that play with symbols and the construction of meaning in an open text that has no design or intention of imposing a hegemonic view or of insisting on its own superiority.

Story, storytelling See Narrative above. An explanation that makes no truth claims but admits to being the teller's point of view based only on his or her experience. Traditional, local narratives are stories.

Subjectivity Used by Postmodernists to refer to an emphasis on the subject as a focus of social analysis. The Postmodernists criticize subjectivity. Postmodernists do not employ this word in its modern sense of philosophical relativism or tentativeness or the opposite of objectivity.

Text All phenomena, all events. Postmodernists consider everything a text.

Totalizing Assumes a totality, a total view. By extension, this rejects other perspectives. Postmodernists criticize totalizing theories.

Voice The modern conception of the author's perspective. Postmodernists question the attribution of privilege or special status to any voice, authors, or a specific person or perspectives. The "public" voice, however, is more acceptable to Postmodernists because it democratizes rhetoric, makes discourse broadly understandable, and at the same time subverts "its own expert culture."[7]

Notes

INTRODUCTION

1 Jeffrey Jensen Arnett, *Emerging Adulthood: The Winding Road from the Late Teens through the Twenties* (Oxford: Oxford University Press, 2004).
2 The term "war for talent" was coined by McKinsey's Steven Hankin in 1997 and popularized by the book of that name in 2001. See Ed Michaels, Helen Handfield-Jones, and Beth Axelrod, *The War for Talent* (Boston: Harvard Business School Publishing, 2001).

CHAPTER ONE

1 "FT_19.01.17_generations_2019_topicArtboard 19 copy 3@2x," Pew Research Center, accessed 2 April 2020, www.pewsocialtrends.org/essay/ Millennial-life-how-young-adulthood-today-compares-with-prior-generations/ft_19-01-17_generations_2019_topicartboard-19-copy-32x-2/.
2 Steven Hankin of McKinsey coined the phrase "the war for talent" in 1997. In 2001, a book with the same title brought the term even more to the fore: Ed Michaels, Helen Handfield-Jones, and Beth Axelrod, *The War for Talent* (Boston: Harvard Business School Press, 2001).
3 Cale Tilford, "The Millennial Moment in Charts," *Financial Times*, 6 June 2018.
4 John Gapper, "How Millennials Became the World's Most Powerful Consumers," *Financial Times*, 5 June 2018.

5 "Health, History, and Hard Choices: Funding Dilemmas in a Fast Changing World," World Health Organization, accessed 23 April 2020, www.who.int/global_health_histories/seminars/presentation07.pdf.
6 "UNdata," United Nations, accessed 23 April 2020, https://data.un.org/.
7 Lynda Gratton and Andrew Scott, *The 100-Year Life: Living and Working in an Age of Longevity* (London: Bloomsbury, 2016).
8 Generation Z will attend more years of college than Millennials – according to the 15 February 2019 article in *Ecampusnews* by Laura Ascione: "Just 25 percent of Generation Z students say they believe they can have a rewarding career without going to college, compared to 40 percent of Millennials."
9 Donald Olding Hebb, *The Organization of Behavior: A Neuropsychological Theory* (Road Hove, UK: Psychology Press, 2005).
10 Raymond Cattell, ed., *Intelligence: Its Structure, Growth, and Action*, Chapter 5, The Discovery of Fluid and Crystallized General Intelligence (Amsterdam: North Holland Publishing, 1987).
11 John Palfrey and Urs Gasser, *Born Digital: Understanding the First Generation of Digital Natives* (New York: Basic Books, 2008).
12 Deloitte, "Deloitte Global Millennials Survey 2018."
13 Gordon Moore, "Cramming More Components onto Integrated Circuits," *Electronics* 38, no. 8 (April 1965).

CHAPTER TWO

1 According to Wikipedia, "*The Jetsons* is an animated sitcom produced by Hanna-Barbera, originally airing in prime-time from 1962–1963 and again from 1985–1987. Reruns can frequently be seen on Boomerang and Cartoon Network."
2 Julian Huxley, *Religion without Revelation* (Westport, CT: Praeger, 1979).
3 Aleysha Haniff, "Transcripts and Audio: Tony Blair on His Faith and Religious Ideology," *Globe and Mail*, August 2012, www.theglobeand mail.com/opinion/munk-debates/transcripts-and-audio-tony-blair-on-his-faith-and-religious-ideology/article598667/.
4 John Micklethwait and Adrian Wooldridge, *God Is Back* (London: Penguin Press, 2009).

5 Heinrich Klotz and Radka Donnell, *The History of Postmodern Architecture* (Boston: The MIT Press, 1988).

6 Eleanor Heartney, *Postmodernism* (Cambridge: Cambridge University Press, 2001).

7 Many books have been written about a movement within contemporary Christianity called the Emerging Church. It is evangelical Christianity trying to reach out to Postmoderns. A good primer on this movement is D.A. Carson's *Becoming Conversant with the Emerging Church: Understanding a Movement and Its Implications* (Grand Rapids, MI: Zondervan, 2005). Typical of Postmodern thought, this movement has its critics: see Kevin DeYoung and Ted Kluck's *Why We're Not Emergent: By Two Guys Who Should Be* (Chicago: Moody Publishers, 2008). A more academic book is John D. Caputo, *What Would Jesus Deconstruct? The Good News of Postmodernity for the Church* (Grand Rapids, MI: Baker Academic, 2007).

8 Sally Banes, *Terpsichore in Sneakers: Post-Modern Dance* (Middleton, CT: Wesleyan University Press, 1987).

9 Much of Postmodern thought emerged out of philosophy and literature studies – many of the big names of Postmodern thought wrote in the area of literature; some of the most influential include the three Frenchmen Michel Foucault, Jean-François Lyotard, and the ubiquitous Jacques Derrida.

10 Hans Bertens, *The Idea of the Postmodern: A History Paperback* (New York: Routledge, 1995); George Edwards, "Music and Postmodernism," *Partisan Review* 58, no. 4 (Fall 1991): 693–705.

11 A rather droll website devoted to the topic is www.postmodernpsychology.com/; we suspect you will enjoy it, as we did, though you may not always agree.

12 Ibid.

13 Peter Lattman, "The Origins of Justice Stewart's 'I Know It When I See It,'" *Wall Street Journal*, 27 September 2007.

CHAPTER THREE

1 Interview with author; by phone, 3 May 2019.

2 Lee Ventola, "Current Issues Regarding Complementary and Alternative Medicine (CAM) in the United States," *Pharmacy and Therapeutics* 35, no. 9 (September 2010): 514–22.

3 Ibid.

4 National Cancer Institute, Health Information National Trends Survey 5, cycle 4 (February–June 2020), question "In the past 12 months, have you used a computer, smartphone, or other electronic means to look for health or medical information for yourself?," https://hints.cancer.gov/view-questions-topics/question-details.aspx?PK_Cycle=13&qid =1606.

5 Pew Research Center, *The Social Life of Health Information* [Fact Sheet], (2009). Available at https://www.pewresearch.org/internet/2009/06/11/the-social-life-of-health-information/.

6 Ibid.

7 Pew Research Center, "Health Fact Sheet," 16 December 2013, www.pew internet.org/fact-sheets/health-fact-sheet/.

8 Eric Silfen, "The Physician-Patient Relationship," *Huffington Post*, 6 August 2013.

9 As discussed in an interview with Professor Karl Moore.

10 Robert M. Carrothers, Stanford W. Gregory Jr, and Timothy J. Gallagher, "Measuring Emotional Intelligence of Medical School Applicants," *Academic Medicine: Journal of the Association of American Medical Colleges* 75, no. 5 (April 2000): 456–63.

CHAPTER FOUR

1 Daniel Levitin, *This Is Your Brain on Music* (Boston: Dutton, 2006). This is an excellent book. It is a pleasure to read, bringing some of the latest neurological research forward and making it accessible to the non-expert. Daniel comes to my leadership class every year, sharing with students his experience as a musician, sound engineer, and record producer, having worked with artists such as Stevie Wonder and Blue Oyster Cult, and how after his PhD from Stanford in neuroscience he became a professor and bestselling author.

2 Ibid.

3   William Davies, "The Age of Post-Truth Politics," *The New York Times*, 24 August 2016.

4   An Edelman vice-chairman, he was speaking at an Edelman-sponsored event, 30 November 2016. He was played by Woody Harrelson in the 2012 HBO movie *Game Change*, about the 2008 US presidential campaign.

5   Peter Baker, "Lies, Damned Lies and Washington," *The New York Times*, 9 December 2019.

6   Pauline Vaillancourt Rosnau, *Post-Modernism and the Social Sciences: Insights, Inroads, and Intrusions* (Princeton, NJ: Princeton University Press, 1992).

7   Quoted in ibid.

8   Ian Katz, "Ian McEwan on His Novels as A-Level Set Texts: 'My Son Got a Very Low Mark,'" *The Guardian*, 3 April 2012, www.guardian.co. uk/books/video/2012/apr/03/ian-mcewan-a-level-set-text-video.

9   Rosenau, *Post-Modernism and the Social Sciences*.

10 Gianpiero Petriglieri, "Emotions Are Data Too," *Harvard Business Review* (May 2014), http://blogs.hbr.org/2014/05/emotions-are-data-too.

11 Ibid.

12 Ibid.

13 Olivia Fox Cabane, *The Charisma Myth: How Anyone Can Master the Art and Science of Personal Magnetism* (London: Portfolio/Penguin Group, 2012).

14 Arlie Russell Hochschild, *The Managed Heart: Commercialization of Human Feeling* (Berkeley: University of California Press, 1982).

15 This is one of the three quotes that Mike shared in my CEO Insights class for MBAS. Each of the twenty-three CEOs that come as guests are asked to bring three quotes that summarize their leadership philosophy, phrases that they would use a number of times a year when talking to their employees to let them know how they want things done. This quote calls to mind Thomas Edison's: "Vision without execution is hallucination."

16 Cameron Anderson and Courtney E. Brown, "The Functions and Dysfunctions of Hierarchy," *Research in Organizational Behavior* 30 (2012): 55–89.

17 Karl Moore, "For Millennials, Thinking and Emotions Are Equal – More or Less," *Forbes*, 26 June 2017.
18 Arlie Hochschild, *The Managed Heart: Commercialization of Human Feeling*, 3rd ed. (Berkeley: University of California Press, 2012).
19 "Emotional Labor," *Wikipedia*, https://en.wikipedia.org/wiki/Emotional _labor, accessed 20 April 2020.
20 Karl Moore, "'Never Apologize, Never Explain' and Other Bad Ideas for Working with Millennials," *Globe and Mail*, 9 January 2018.
21 Quy Huy, "Scaling Up Emotional Intelligence to Inspire the Crowd," *INSEAD*, 30 March 2016. https://knowledge.insead.edu/blog/insead-blog/scaling-up-emotional-intelligence-to-inspire-the-crowd-4607.
22 In an interview with the author for the *National Post*, 24 July 2017. Part of the interview was published in https://business.financialpost.com/ executive/what-a-new-york-times-columnist-learned-from-interview ing-ceos.
23 John Ibbitson, *Open & Shut: Why America Has Barack Obama, and Canada Has Stephen Harper* (Toronto: McClelland & Stewart, 2009).
24 Alan Kirby, "The Death of Postmodernism and Beyond," *Philosophy Now*, 2006.

CHAPTER FIVE

1 Marshall Goldsmith, "Five Global Leadership Factors," *Bloomberg*, 13 October 2009, www.bloomberg.com/news/articles/2009-10-13/five-global-leadership-factors.
2 Francisco J. García-Peñalvo and Nicholas Alfred Kearney, "Networked Youth Research for Empowerment in Digital Society. The WYRED Project" (TEEM'16, Salamanca, Spain, 2019).
3 Jozef Wilezynski, *An Encyclopedic Dictionary of Marxism, Socialism and Communism* (Berlin: Walter de Gruyter GmbH & Co KG, 2019).
4 Cuba and North Korea are still somewhat Communist nations. China is, too, but it seems to be rather good at beating the United States and other countries on the competitive capitalist field.
5 Maria Ivanova-Gongne and Jan-Åke Törnroos, "Understanding Cultural Sensemaking of Business Interaction: A Research Model," *Scandinavian Journal of Management* 33, no. 2 (2017): 102–12.

6   Arthur Zaezkiewiez, "Listen Up: What It Takes to Manage Millennials," *Women's Wear Daily*, 21 September 2016.

7   Ibid.

8   Darlene Andert et al., "The Millennial Effect: A Multi-Generational Leadership Model," *International Leadership Journal* 11, no. 2 (2019): 32–63.

9   Jaso L. Frand, "The Information-Age Mindset," *Educause Review*, 1 January 2000, 14–24.

10 Nick Gillespie and Emily Ekins, "Generation Independent," *Reason Magazine*, 14 October 2014.

11 Diana Oblinger, "Boomers, Gen-Xers and Millennials: Understanding the New Students," *Educause Review*, 1 January 2003, 37–47.

12 Peter Groves et al., "The 'Big Data' Revolution in Healthcare: Accelerating Value and Innovation," *McKinsey Quarterly*, April 2013.

13 Henry Mintzberg, "Enough of Silos? How about Slabs?," 22 October 2015, www.mintzberg.org/blog/slabs.

14 Henry Mintzberg, *Managing* (San Francisco: Berrett-Koehler Publishers, 2009).

15 Greg L. Stewart, "A Meta-Analytic Review of Relationships between Team Design Features and Team Performance," *Journal of Management* 32, no. 1 (January 2006): 29–55.

16 Karen A. Bantel and Susan E. Jackson, "Top Management and Innovations in Banking: Does the Composition of the Top Team Make a Difference?," *Strategic Management Journal* 10, no. S1 (Summer, 1989): 107–24.

17 "'It's about More Than One Individual's Success': Indigenous Leaders Share Their Stories, Strategies and Life Lessons," *Globe and Mail*, 22 April 2021, www.theglobeandmail.com/business/article-its-about-more-than-one-individuals-success-indigenous-leaders-share/.

18 Harry C. Triandis, Lois L. Kurowski, and Michele J. Gelfand, "Workplace Diversity," *Handbook of Industrial and Organizational Psychology* 4, no. 2 (Palo Alto, CA: Consulting Psychology Press, 1994): 769–827. An excellent book on the topic of introverted leaders is *Quiet*, by Susan Cain (New York: Random House, 2013). Susan is an outstanding writer and not an academic researcher but does an excellent job of presenting solid academic ideas in an accessible manner.

19 Rosabeth Moss Kanter, *Think Outside the Building: How Advanced Leaders Can Change the World One Smart Innovation at a Time* (New York: PublicAffairs, 2020).

20 Isabelle Hudon, interview by Karl Moore, *The CEO Series*, Bell Media (CJAD 800). Accessed 24 April 2020, https://soundcloud.com/cjad800/martine-turcotte-isabelle-hudon-ceo-series-dec-11.

21 Christopher C. Gearhart and Graham D. Bodie, "Active-Empathic Listening as a General Social Skill: Evidence from Bivariate and Canonical Correlations," *Journal Communication Reports* 24, no. 2 (October 2011): 86–98.

22 Niels Van Quaquebeke and Will Felps, "Respectful Inquiry: A Motivational Account of Leading through Asking Questions and Listening," *Academy of Management Review* 43, no. 1 (2018): 1–23.

23 Michael E. Porter, "What Is Strategy?" *Harvard Business Review* 74, no. 6 (November–December 1996): 61–78.

24 Henry Mintzberg, *Managing* (San Francisco: Berrett-Koehler Publishers, 2009).

25 Janie Smith, "What HR Can Learn from Bill Clinton, the Albert Einstein of Listening," *Human Resources Director*, 15 April 2014.

26 Amy Jen Su and Muriel Maignan Wilkins, "What Gets in the Way of Listening," *Harvard Business Review*, 14 April 2014, https://hbr.org/2014/04/what-gets-in-the-way-of-listening.

27 Sara Stibitz, "How to Really Listen to Your Employees," *Harvard Business Review*, web article, 29 January 2015.

28 Su and Wilkins, "What Gets in the Way of Listening."

29 Peter Goldberg, "Change Module," Lecture, International Masters for Health Leadership (McGill University, Montreal, 20 July 2016).

30 David F. Larcker et al., *2013 CEO Performance Evaluation Survey* (The Miles Group and Stanford University, May 2013).

31 Ibid.

32 Ibid.

33 Laura Janusik, n.d, *Listening Facts*, accessed 1 January 2020, http://d10 25403.site.myhosting.com/files.listen.org/Facts.htm#References.

34 Melissa Daimler, "Listening Is an Overlooked Leadership Tool," *Harvard Business Review*, web article, 24 May 2016.

35 Daniel Lamarre, interview by Karl Moore, *The CEO Series*, Bell Media

(CJAD 800), accessed 24 April 2020, https://soundcloud.com/cjad800/daniel-lamarre-ceo-series-apr-1.

36 Ram Charan, "The Discipline of Listening," *Harvard Business Review*, 21 June 2012, https://hbr.org/2012/06/the-discipline-of-listening.

37 For an overview of some of the author's research on Quiet or Introverted Leaders, see Kate Rodriguez, "Leaders, Consider Your Introverts," *The Economist*, accessed 18 April 2020, https://execed.economist.com/career-advice/career-hacks/leaders-consider-your-introverts.

38 Melissa Daimler, "Listening Is an Overlooked Leadership Tool," *Harvard Business Review*, web article, 25 May 2016.

39 Sherry Turkle, *Reclaiming Conversation: The Power of Talk in a Digital Age* (New York: Penguin Press, 2015).

40 Daimler, "Listening Is an Overlooked Leadership Tool."

41 Christopher C. Gearhart and Graham D. Bodie, "Active-Empathic Listening as a General Social Skill: Evidence from Bivariate and Canonical Correlations," *Communication Reports* 24, no. 2 (2011): 86–98.

42 Christine M. Riordan, "Three Ways Leaders Can Listen with More Empathy," *Harvard Business Review*, 16 January 2014, https://hbr.org/2014/01/three-ways-leaders-can-listen-with-more-empathy.

43 Mark Bowden, *Winning Body Language* (New York: McGraw Hill Books, 2010).

44 Riordan, "Three Ways Leaders Can Listen."

45 Ram Charan, "The Discipline of Listening," *Harvard Business Review*, 21 June 2012, https://hbr.org/2012/06/the-discipline-of-listening.

46 Riordan, "Three Ways Leaders Can Listen."

47 Ibid.

48 Karl Moore, "Leadership Lessons from a Four-Star General," *The Globe and Mail*, 11 August 2009, www.theglobeandmail.com/report-on-business/careers/leadership-lessons-from-a-four-star-general/article4281436.

49 One day, Henry Mintzberg and I were working in his office and a colleague of ours called from London where she had just gotten out of a meeting where Bill Clinton had spoken. We have never heard her so excited and enthusiastic about someone – especially considering that she is a frugal type who you wouldn't expect would spend the kind of money you'd need to call Montreal from a London cab on your

Canadian cell phone. A few years ago, McGill University gave Clinton an honorary doctorate, and people raved for months afterward about him. He seems to have that effect on people.

50 Bernard Ferrari, *Power Listening: Mastering the Most Critical Business Skill of All* (New York: Penguin Group, 2012).

51 Boris Groysberg and Michael Slind, *Talk Inc.* (Boston: Harvard Business School Publishing, 2012).

52 Inga Jona Jonsdottir and Kristrun Fridriksdottir, "Active Listening: Is It the Forgotten Dimension in Managerial Communication?" *International Journal of Listening* 34, no. 3 (May 2019), https://doi.org/10.1080/10904018.2019.1613156.

CHAPTER SIX

1 Donna Ladkin and Chellie Spiller, *Authentic Leadership: Clashes, Convergences, and Coalescences* (Northampton, MA: Edward Elgar Publishing Inc., 2013).

2 Charles Guignon, "Hermeneutics, Authenticity and the Aims of Psychology," *Journal of Theoretical and Philosophical Psychology* 22, no. 2 (2002): 83–102.

3 Clark Wolff Hamel, "Facebook, Twitter, Gender: How Social Media Allows for Fragmentation of the Self in the Digitally Native Millennial," Bard College senior project, spring 2017, https://digitalcommons.bard.edu/senproj_s2017/369.

4 Jacob Golomb, *In Search of Authenticity: Existentialism from Kierkegaard to Camus* (New York: Routledge, 1995).

5 Ibid.

6 The author has had the pleasure of interviewing MIT's Edward Schien, the "father" of corporate culture studies; you can see the interviews on the author's YouTube channel at www.youtube.com/watch?v=hasd KAhXhZg and www.youtube.com/watch?v=ooj7Z21-oA. Both reflect Schien's thinking about corporate culture.

7 The term "organization man" comes from the best seller, *The Organization Man* by William H. Whyte, published by Simon & Schuster in 1956.

Whyte, a writer for *Fortune* magazine, introduced the term to the popular lexicon. Another book from the same era, *The Man in the Gray Flannel Suit*, by Sloan Wilson, published by Simon & Schuster, is a novel about the search for purpose in the corporate world of that time. Though corporations have evolved very considerably since then, they still have a tendency to squeeze people into a corporate culture and, at their worst moments, make us feel like cogs in a machine. Certainly, when the author worked for IBM this was his experience, and in his executive teaching, he often encounters a sense of alienation that some have because of the pressures of corporate life – pressures that Millennials understandably, given their parents' experience, often resist.

8 Lynne Lancaster and David Stillman, *When Generations Collide: Who They Are. Why They Clash. How To Solve the Generational Puzzle at Work* (New York: Harper Business, 2003).

9 Stanley Milgram, *Obedience to Authority: An Experimental View* (New York: Harper & Row, 1974).

10 For one, see Jerry M. Burger, "Replicating Milgram: Would People Still Obey Today?," *American Psychologist* 64 (2009): 1–11; Alison Abbott, "Modern Milgram Experiment Sheds Light on Power of Authority," *Nature* 530, no. 7591 (January 2016): 394–5.

11 Michelle Eggleston, *Millennials Want Passionate Leaders* (30 December 2013), Training Industry, accessed 17 October 2016, www.trainingindus try.com/blog/blog-entries/Millennials-want-passionate-leaders.aspx.

12 Bruce J. Avolio and William L. Gardner, "Authentic Leadership Development: Getting to the Root of Positive Forms of Leadership," *The Leadership Quarterly* 16 (2005): 315–38.

13 Steve Cody, "5 Tricks for Working with Millennials," *Inc.*, 18 April 2013.

14 Robert Ruzzuto, "TEDx Springfield Talks Promote Innovation through Diversity," *MassLive*, October 2013, www.masslive.com/news/index.ssf/ 2013/10/tedx_springfield_talks_promote.html.

15 Jon Morris, "The Y Factor: How to Nurture Star Qualities in Millennials," *Inc.*, 17 October 2013.

16 Felix Salmon, "Why Salaries Shouldn't Be Secret," LinkedIn Pulse, 15 May 2014, www.linkedin.com/pulse/20140515050804-10400206-why-salaries-shouldn-t-be-secret.

17 Kevin Kruse, "What Is Authentic Leadership?," *Forbes.com*, 12 May 2013, www.forbes.com/sites/kevinkruse/2013/05/12/what-is-authentic-leadership/#551aab6d2ddd.

18 Ibid.

19 Ibid.; Yusuf M. Sidani and W. Glenn Rowe, "A Reconceptualization of Authentic Leadership: Leader Legitimation Via Follower-Centered Assessment of the Moral Dimension," *The Leadership Quarterly* 29, no. 6 (2018): 623–36.

20 Kruse, "What Is Authentic Leadership?"

CHAPTER SEVEN

1 "How Millennials Want to Work and Live," Washington, DC: Gallup, Inc., accessed 24 April 2020, www.gallup.com/workplace/238073/Millennials-work-live.aspx.

2 Bruce N. Pfau and Ira T. Kay, *The Human Capital Edge* (New York: McGraw-Hill, 2001).

3 Bruce N. Pfau, "What Do Millennials Really Want at Work? The Same Things the Rest of Us Do," *Harvard Business Review*, 7 April 2016.

4 Ibid.

5 John J. Heldrich Center for Workforce Development, *Talent Report: What Workers Want in 2012*, Net Impact (New Brunswick, NJ: Rutgers, The State University of New Jersey), www.netimpact.org/whatworkers want.

6 Carolyn Heller Baird, "Myths, Exaggerations and Uncomfortable Truths: The Real Story behind Millennials in the Workplace," IBM Institute for Business Value (2015), accessed 24 April 2020, www.ibm.com/downloads/cas/Q3ZVGRLP.

7 "Heartland Monitor Poll #22: Americans' Local Experiences," *The Allstate/National Journal Heartland Monitor Polling Series*, 2015.

8 Ibid.

9 Ibid.; 57 per cent of the Millennials polled mentioned one of these two motivation factors.

10 Deloitte Touche Tohmatsu Limited, "The 2016 Deloitte Millennial Survey."

11 Deloitte Touche Tohmatsu Limited, "The 2016 Deloitte Millennial Survey."
12 "How Millennials Want to Work and Live."
13 Ibid.
14 Charles Donkor and Alina Slobodjanjuk, "Millennials in the Hospitality, Aviation and Business Travel Industry," World Tourism Forum Lucerne, 17–19 April 2013, accessed 24 April 2020, https://static1.square space.com/static/56dacbc6d210b821510cf939/t/57ab4e4d59cc68ea5de38ff d/1470844494321/Millennials+in+the+Hospitality%2C+Aviation+and+Business+Travel+Industry.pdf.
15 Gail Johnson, "Millennials Need Purpose, Not Ping-Pong," *The Globe and Mail*, 23 March 2016, www.theglobeandmail.com/report-on-busi ness/Millennials-need-purpose-not-ping-pong/article29337726/.
16 Geoff Molson, interview by Karl Moore, *The CEO Series*, Bell Media (CJAD 800), accessed 24 April 2020, https://soundcloud.com/cjad800/ geoff-molson-ceo-series-nov-8.
17 Tessa Basford and Bill Schaninger, "Winning Hearts and Minds in the 21st Century," *McKinsey Quarterly*, April 2016, 122–6.
18 Donkor and Slobodjanjuk, "Millennials in the Hospitality, Aviation and Business Travel Industry."
19 Deloitte Touche Tohmatsu Limited, "The 2016 Deloitte Millennial Survey."
20 Ibid.
21 Ibid.
22 Ibid.
23 "How Millennials Want to Work and Live."
24 Deloitte Touche Tohmatsu Limited, "The 2016 Deloitte Millennial Survey."
25 Basford and Schaninger, "Winning Hearts and Minds."
26 Deloitte Touche Tohmatsu Limited, "The 2016 Deloitte Millennial Survey."
27 Adam Smiley Poswolsky, "4 Tips to Help Millennials Find Meaningful Work," *Fast Company*, 16 April 2014, www.fastcompany.com/3029111/4-tips-to-help-Millennials-find-meaningful-work.
28 Johnson, "Millennials Need Purpose."

29 Jeanne Meister, "Job Hopping Is the 'New Normal' for Millennials: Three Ways to Prevent a Human-Resource Nightmare," *Forbes.com*, 14 August 2012, www.forbes.com/sites/jeannemeister/2012/08/14/the-future-of-work-job-hopping-is-the- new-normal-for-Millennials/#5ce0ec4a13b8.

30 Poswolsky, "4 Tips to Help Millennials."

31 Karl Moore, "Patrick Pichette: 'When Work Starts Feeling Too Comfortable, Fire Yourself,'" *The Globe and Mail*, 5 September 2016.

32 John Wood, interview by Karl Moore, *The* CEO *Series*, Bell Media (CJAD 800), accessed 24 April 2020, https://soundcloud.com/cjad800/john-wood-ceo-series-jan-15.

33 Karl Moore, "John Wood: 'I Had to Get Out of Microsoft and Make Education for the World's Poorest Children My Job,'" *National Post*, 19 January 2016, http://business.financialpost.com/executive/leader ship/john-wood-i-had-to-get-out-of-microsoft-and-make-education-for-the-worlds-poorest-children-my-job.

34 The Hot Cities Tour of the World trip has visited Israel, the UAE, India, South Africa, Russia, Mongolia/South Korea, Jakarta and Bali, Chile and Colombia, the Philippines, Malaysia, and, most recently, Tokyo/Bangkok and Hong Kong. Based on the predictions of the *Economist* Intelligence Unit, students choose a destination and spend eleven days meeting with a dozen CEOs from businesses and NGOs, as well as with government and political leaders. The slogan of the trip is "Taking the Future to the Future," that is, taking young people to where the future economy may be going. Unfortunately, our 2020 trip to Vietnam and Seoul was cancelled two days before we were to leave due to the COVID-19 pandemic. In 2023 we are off to Ghana and the Côte d'Ivoire.

35 In discussing this with MBAS in their late thirties and early forties, the author has heard a number of times that friends from the same MBA program who went into the civil society sector are often bitter by this point in their careers – ten or more years in – about the realities of working for an NGO, where petty arguments, politics, and driven behaviour can all be found.

36 Nick Lovegrove and Matthew Thomas, "21st Century Leadership: The Tri-Sector Athlete," *Global-is-Asian* 15 (Oct–December 2010): 36–40.

37 "How Millennials Want to Work and Live."

38 Leah Eichler, "For Younger Workers, Perks Trump Pay," *The Globe and Mail*, 13 September 2013.

39 Ibid.

40 Russel Calk and Angela Patrick, "Millennials through the Looking Glass: Workplace Motivating Factors," *The Journal of Business Inquiry* 16, no. 2 (2017): 131–9.

41 Patrik Frisk, interview by Karl Moore, *The* CEO *Series*, Bell Media (CJAD 800), accessed 24 April 2020, https://soundcloud.com/cjad800/patrik-frisk-ceo-series-feb-19.

42 Dan Pontefract, *The Purpose Effect* (Boise, ID: Elevate, 2016).

43 Ibid.

44 Ibid.

45 Ibid.

46 Ibid.

47 Deloitte Touche Tohmatsu Limited, "The 2016 Deloitte Millennial Survey."

48 Ibid.

49 Pontefract, *The Purpose Effect*.

50 Richard J. Leider, *The Power of Purpose: Find Meaning, Live Longer, Better*, 3rd ed. (Oakland, CA: Berrett-Koehler Publishers, 2018).

51 Ibid.

52 Robert H. Frank, "The Incalculable Value of Finding a Job You Love," *The New York Times*, 22 July 2016.

53 Deloitte Touche Tohmatsu Limited, "The 2016 Deloitte Millennial Survey."

54 Ibid.

55 Ibid.

56 Ibid.

57 Deloitte, "The Deloitte Global Millennial Survey 2019."

58 Ibid.

59 Basford and Schaninger, "Winning Hearts and Minds."

60 Joanna Barsh, Lauren Brown, and Kayvan Kian, "Millennials: Burden, Blessing, or Both?," *McKinsey Quarterly* (February 2016): 127–31.

61 Ibid.

62 This quote is from www.ibm.com/ibm/responsibility/corporateservice corps.

63 Spencer E. Ante, "Offering Advice Free of Charge," *Wall Street Journal*, 6 December 2010, http://online.wsj.com/news/articles/SB1000142405 27487033501045756532442220509622. Learn more about the program at www.ibm.com/ibm/responsibility/corporateservicecorps.

64 Eric Friedman, interview by Karl Moore, *The* CEO *Series*, Bell Media (CJAD 800), accessed 24 April 2020, https://soundcloud.com/cjad800/ eric-friedman-podcast.

65 D. Schawbel, "10 Ways Millennials Are Creating the Future of Work," *Forbes.com*, 16 December 2013, www.forbes.com/sites/danschawbel/ 2013/12/16/10-ways-Millennials-are-creating-the-future-of-work/# 56908f463105.

66 Francesca Colantuoni et al., "A Fresh Look at Paternity Leave: Why the Benefits Extend beyond the Personal," *McKinsey & Company*, 5 March 2021, www.mckinsey.com/business-functions/people-and-organiza tional-performance/our-insights/a-fresh-look-at-paternity-leave-why- the-benefits-extend-beyond-the-personal.

67 Barsh, Brown, and Kian, "Millennials: Burden, Blessing, or Both?"

68 Sheelah Kolhatkar, "Men Are People Too," *BusinessWeek Magazine*, 30 March 2013.

69 Please see McKinsey & Company's website for more details: www. mckinsey.com/careers/a_place_to_grow/work_life_journey.

70 Basford and Schaninger, "Winning Hearts and Minds."

71 Daisuke Wakabayashi and Steve Lohr, "Bill Gates Stepping Down from Microsoft's Board," *The New York Times*, 13 March 2020, www.nytimes. com/2020/03/13/technology/bill-gates-microsoft-board.html.

CHAPTER EIGHT

1 Cale Tilford, "The Millennial Moment in Charts," *Financial Times*, 6 June 2018.

2 Barbara A. Friedberg, "Are We in a Baby Boomer Retirement Crisis?" *Investopedia*, 23 September 2019, www.investopedia.com/articles/ personal-finance/032216/are-we-baby-boomer-retirement-crisis.asp.

3 Lauren Brousell, "6 Ways to Give Millennials the Mentorship Programs

They Want," *CIO*, 16 July 2015, https://www.cio.com/article/244528/6-ways-to-give-millennials-the-mentorship-programs-they-want.html.
4 Kathy E. Kram and Monica C. Higgins, "A New Approach to Mentoring," *The Wall Street Journal*, 22 September 2008.
5 Brousell, "6 Ways."
6 Marina Khidekel, "The Misery of Mentoring Millennials," *Bloomberg Business*, 3 March 2013.
7 Karie Willyerd, "Millennials Want to Be Coached at Work," *Harvard Business Review*, 27 February 2015, https://hbr.org/2015/02/millennials-want-to-be-coached-at-work.
8 Jeanne C. Meister and Karie Willyerd, "Mentoring Millennials," *Harvard Business Review*, May 2010, 12–17.
9 Ibid.
10 Ibid.
11 Ibid.
12 Dan Schawbel, "How Millennials Will Shape the Future of Work," *Pando*, 3 September 2013.
13 Willyerd, "Millennials Want to Be Coached."
14 Ibid.
15 Dan Schawbel, "Millennials vs Baby Boomers: Who Would You Rather Hire?," *Time Magazine*, 29 March 2012.
16 Willyerd, "Millennials Want to Be Coached."
17 Amy Gallo, "Demystifying Mentoring," *Harvard Business Review*, 1 February 2011, https://hbr.org/2011/02/demystifying-mentoring.
18 Ilan Mochari, "3 Tips for Mentoring Millennials," *Inc.*, 7 February 2014, https://www.inc.com/ilan-mochari/3-tips-mentoring-millennials.html.
19 Ibid.
20 Brousell, "6 Ways."
21 Jeremy Boudinet, "What Millennials Really Need (Hint: It's Not Feedback)," *The Muse*, 2015.
22 Ibid.
23 Ibid.
24 Gallo, "Demystifying Mentoring."
25 Karl Moore and Sienna Zampino, "Working with Millennials – Why You Need to Listen More and Talk Less," *Forbes.com*, 8 July 2014,

https://www.forbes.com/sites/karlmoore/2014/07/08/working-with-millennials-why-you-need-to-listen-more-and-talk-less.

26 Arihant Patni, "Mentorship in 2019: Future Course & How Things Have Changed," *LinkedIn Pulse*, 27 February 2019.

27 Ibid.

28 Khidekel, "The Misery of Mentoring Millennials."

29 Brousell, "6 Ways."

30 Ibid.

31 Amrita Singh, "Tell Me and I Forget, Teach Me and I May Remember, Involve Me and I Learn – Benji Franklin," *LinkedIn Pulse*, 19 May 2016, https://www.linkedin.com/pulse/tell-me-i-forget-teach-may-remember-involve-learn-benji-singh/.

32 Deloitte, "The Deloitte Global Millennial Survey 2019."

33 There is an excellent short video where Jack Welch, CEO, talks about how he learned about reverse mentoring and how he quickly brought it to GE and tipped the organization upside down. "Reverse Mentoring," YouTube, 14 September 2013, www.youtube.com/watch?v=Pux4oFNW9lk (@coachkriengsak).

34 This is some excellent advice from a couple of researchers at IMD. Jennifer Jorden and Michael Sorell, "Why Reverse Mentoring Works and How to Do It Right," *Harvard Business Review*, 3 October 2019.

35 I have two beloved older mentors; they have been enormously useful over the years, but I don't think it would occur to them to ask for my advice. It is something simply not done in their day.

36 Shaun Hunter, as quoted in Dawn Wood, "Reverse Mentoring Gives Gen Y a Boost of Confidence," *The Globe and Mail*, updated 11 May 2018.

37 Ibid.

38 Karl Moore and Sienna Zampino, "The Modern Mentor in a Millennial Workplace," *Forbes.com*, 11 September 2014.

39 Moore and Zampino, "Working with Millennials."

40 Deloitte, "The Deloitte Global Millennial Survey 2018."

41 Jorden and Sorell, "Why Reverse Mentoring Works."

42 Emma De Vita, "Reverse Mentoring: What Young Women Can Teach the Old Guard," *Financial Times*, 6 March 2019.

43 HRD, "Inside PwC's Reverse Mentoring Program," *Human Resources Director*, 4 October 2018.
44 Jorden and Sorell, "Why Reverse Mentoring Works."
45 Heather McGregor, "Tap the Wisdom of Junior Colleagues," *Financial Times*, 28 March 2022.
46 Estée Lauder, "Learning and Development," accessed 14 November 2022, www.elcompanies.com/en/careers/why-work-here/learning-and-development.
47 Jennifer Jordan and Michael Sorell, "Why You Should Create a Shadow Board of Younger Employees," *Harvard Business Review*, 4 June 2019.
48 Khidekel, "The Misery of Mentoring Millennials."
49 Willyerd, "Millennials Want to Be Coached."

CHAPTER NINE

1 Amy Glass, "Understanding Generational Differences for Competitive Success," *Industrial and Commercial Training* 39, no. 2 (2007): 98–103.
2 Jeanne C. Meister and Karie Willyerd, "Mentoring Millennials," *Harvard Business Review* 88, no. 5 (2010).
3 Sue Shaw and David Fairhurst, "Engaging a New Generation of Graduates," *Education + Training* 50, no. 5 (2008): 366–78.
4 Eddy S.W. Ng, Linda Schweitzer, and Sean T. Lyons, "New Generation, Great Expectations: A Field Study of the Millennial Generation," *Journal of Business and Psychology* 25, no. 2 (2010): 281–92.
5 Kindrick C. Patterson, "Generational Diversity – The Impact of Generational Diversity in the Workplace," *The Diversity Factor* 15, no. 3 (2007): 17–22.
6 Andrea Hershatter and Molly Epstein, "Millennials and the World of Work: An Organization and Management Perspective," *Journal of Business and Psychology* 25, no. 2 (2010): 211–23.
7 Jean Twenge et al., "Generational Differences in Work Values: Leisure and Extrinsic Values Increasing, Social and Intrinsic Values Decreasing," *Journal of Management* 36, no. 5 (2010): 1117–42.
8 Kathryn Tyler, "The Tethered Generation," *HR Magazine* 52, no. 5 (2007): 40–7.

9   Deborah J. Laible, Gustavo Carlo, and Marcela Raffaelli, "The Differential Relations of Parent and Peer Attachment to Adolescent Adjustment," *Journal of Youth and Adolescence: A Multidisciplinary Research Publication* 29, no. 1 (2000): 45–59.

10 Amitia Etzioni, "Social Norms: Internalization, Persuasion, and History," *Law and Society Review* 34, no. 1 (2000): 157–78.

11 Ibid.

12 Sherry L. Clausing et al., "Generational Diversity – the Nexters," *AORN Journal* 78, no. 3 (2003): 373–9.

13 Richard Sweeney, "Millennial Behaviors and Demographics," New Jersey Institute of Technology, revised 22 December 2006, http:// msbasa.weebly.com/uploads/2/6/8/5/26853740/article-millennial-behaviors.pdf, 10.

14 Diane Thielfoldt and Devon Scheef, "Generation X and the Millennials: What You Need to Know about Mentoring the New Generations," *Law Practice Today*, 2004, 1–4.

15 Russell Calk and Angela Patrick, "Millennials through the Looking Glass: Workplace Motivating Factors," *The Journal of Business Inquiry* 16, no. 2 (2017): 131–9.

16 Thielfoldt and Scheef, "Generation X and the Millennials."

17 Stone and Heen's calculation in their book *Thanks for the Feedback* is as follows: American schoolchildren between the ages of six and seventeen, from kindergarten to their high school graduation, spend an average of 3 hours and 58 minutes on homework daily (www.smith sonianmag.com/arts-culture/Do-Kids-Have-Too-Much-Home work.html), and the average school year is 180 days (www.nces.ed.gov/ surveys/pss/tables/table_15.asp). They assume one or two daily assignments as well as term papers, quizzes, mid-terms, finals, and standardized tests are returned to students each year. They estimate approximately 300 assignments are returned – a particularly high number for high school students. In our experience, it is not that much different, if at all, in Canada.

18 Jennifer J. Deal, David G. Altman, and Steven G. Rogelberg, "Millennials at Work: What We Know and What We Need to Do (If Anything)," *Journal of Business and Psychology* 25, no. 2 (2010): 191–9.

19   Laura Pappano, "The Master's as the New Bachelor's," *The New York Times*, 22 July 2011.

20   Joseph Gigante, Michael Dell, and Angela Sharkey, "Getting Beyond 'Good Job': How to Give Effective Feedback," *Pediatrics* 127, no. 2 (2011): 205–7; Charles Thompson and Jane Brodie Gregory, "Managing Millennials: A Framework for Improving Attraction, Motivation, and Retention," *The Psychologist-Manager Journal* 15, no. 4 (2012): 237–46.

21   Mary Madden et al., "Teens and Technology 2013," Pew Research Center, 13 March 2013, https://www.pewresearch.org/internet/wp-content/uploads/sites/9/media/Files/Reports/2013/PIP_Teensand Technology2013.pdf.

22   Ibid.

23   Antoinette Alexander, "Market Strategies Study: Millennial Shoppers Trust Social Media More but Diversify beyond Facebook," *Market Strategies International*, 10 June 2014.

24   Thielfoldt and Scheef, "Generation X and the Millennials."

25   Leslie Altimier, "Leading a New Generation," *Newborn and Infant Nursing Reviews* 6, no. 1 (2006): 7–9.

26   Karen S. Hill, "Defy the Decades with Multigenerational Teams," *Nursing Management* 35, no. 1 (2004): 32–5.

27   Wendy Holliday and Qin Li, "Understanding the Millennials: Updating Our Knowledge about Students," *Reference Services Review* 32, no. 4 (2004): 356–66.

28   Brittany Hite, "Employers Rethink How They Give Feedback," *The Wall Street Journal*, 13 October 2008.

29   Ibid.

30   Samuel Culbert and Lawrence Rout, *Get Rid of the Performance Review* (New York: Hachette Book Group, 2010).

31   Ibid.

32   Ibid.

33   Ibid.

34   David Lee, "What We Can Learn about Feedback from Managing Millennials (& Felons!)," *TLNT*, 8 March 2012.

35   Gary Chapman and Paul White, *The 5 Languages of Appreciation in the Workplace: Empowering Organizations by Encouraging People*, Moody (Chicago: Northfield Publishing, 2019).

36 Paul White, "Generational Differences in the 5 Languages of Apprecia-
    tion," *Appreciation at Work*, 8 May 2014, www.appreciationatwork.com/
    blog/generational-differences-5-languages-appreciation/.
37 Karl Moore, "Five Ways to Give Great Feedback to Millennials,"
    Forbes.com, 20 August 2015.
38 Thomas J. DeLong, "Three Questions for Effective Feedback," *Harvard
    Business Review*, 4 August 2011.
39 Joanne G. Sujansky,"Don't Be So Touchy! The Secrets for Giving
    Feedback to Millennials," *SuperVision* 70, no. 12 (2009).
40 Karl Moore and Sema Burney, "Giving S.M.A.R.T. Feedback to
    Millennials," *Forbes.com*, 4 December 2014.
41 Brittany Hite, "Employers Rethink How They Give Feedback," *The Wall
    Street Journal*, 13 October 2008.
42 Christopher Muther, "The Growing Culture of Impatience Makes
    Us Crave More and More Instant Gratification," *The Boston Globe*,
    2 February 2013.
43 Ibid.
44 Joel A. Garfinkle, *Getting Ahead: Three Steps to Take Your Career to the
    Next Level* (New Jersey: Wiley, 2011).

CHAPTER TEN

1 The Pew Research Center first called them Post-Millennials in a 2018
   look at them. Thankfully they now have their own name: Generation Z
   seems to be the hands-down winner. "Early Benchmarks Show Post-
   Millennials on Track to Be Most Diverse, Best Educated Generation
   Yet," Pew Research Center, 15 November 2018, www.pewsocialtrends.
   org/2018/11/15/early-benchmarks-show-post-Millennials-on-track-to-
   be-most-diverse-best-educated-generation-yet/.
2 The much more negative term "snowflake generation" was one of
   Collins Dictionary's 2016 words of the year. Thankfully that name has
   dropped out of the popular lexicon. "Top 10 Collins Words of the
   Year 2016," *Collins English Dictionary*, 3 November 2016, www.collins
   dictionary.com/word-lovers-blog/new/top-10-collins-words-of-the
   -year-2016,323,HCB.html.

3 Michael Dimock, "Defining Generations: Where Millennials End, and Generation Z Begins," Pew Research Center, 17 January 2019, www.pewresearch.org/fact-tank/2019/01/17/where-Millennials-end-and-generation-z-begins/.

4 Economist Data Team, "Generation Z Is Stressed, Depressed and Exam-Obsessed," *The Economist*, Daily Chart, 27 February 2019.

5 Chris Merrick, "X, Y, Z – Generations in the Workforce," *Training Journal*, 22 June 2016.

6 Tracy Francis, "'True Gen': Generation Z and Its Implication for Companies," McKinsey & Company, November 2018, www.mckinsey.com/industries/consumer-packaged-goods/our-insights/true-gen-generation-z-and-its-implications-for-companies.

7 Marcie Merriman, "The Next Big Disruptor: Gen Z," EY, 2015, www.ey.com/Publication/vwLUAssets/EY-rise-of-gen-znew-challenge-for-retailers/%24FILE/EY-rise-of-gen-znew-challenge-for-retailers.pdf.

8 Richard Fry, "Millennials Projected to Overtake Baby Boomers as America's Largest Generation," Pew Research Center, 1 March 2018.

9 Deloitte Touche Tohmatsu Limited, "The 2016 Deloitte Millennial Survey."

10 Karl Moore, "Porter or Mintzberg: Whose View of Strategy Is the Most Relevant Today?" *Forbes*, 28 March 2011.

11 Henry Mitzenberg, *The Rise and Fall of Strategic Planning* (New York: Free Press, 1994).

12 Jeff Sommer, "A Crisis That Markets Can't Grasp," *The New York Times*, 19 March 2011.

13 Julian Vigo, "Generation Z and New Technology's Effect on Culture," *Forbes*, 2019, www.forbes.com/sites/julianvigo/2019/08/31/generation-z-and-new-technologys-effect-on-culture/#7c175cdb5c2a.

14 "'We're Not Lazy, We're Innovative' – Generation Z Hits Back in Live Debate," BBC, 26 September 2017, www.bbc.co.uk/newsbeat/article/41348207/were-not-lazy-were-innovative—generation-z-hits-back-in-live-debate.

15 Merriman, "The Next Big Disruptor."

16 Tyler Mondres, "How Generation Z Is Changing Financial Services," *ABA Banking Journal*, 3 January 2019.

17 Bharat Chillakuri and Rajendra Mahanandia, "Generation Z Entering

the Workforce," *Human Resource Management International Digest* 26, no. 4 (2018): 34–8.

18 Mondres, "How Generation Z Is Changing Financial Services."

19 Tiffany Mawhinney, "Understanding Gen Z in the Workplace," Deloitte, 2022.

20 Jared Lindzon, "How Do You Become an Employer of Choice?," *The Globe and Mail*, 12 May 2018.

21 Merrick, "X, Y, Z."

22 Mondres, "How Generation Z Is Changing Financial Services."

23 Ibid.

24 Please visit the Susan Cain's Quiet Revolution website for a number of articles on my research: "Karl Moore," *Quiet Revolution*, www.quiet rev.com/author/karl-moore/.

25 Chillakuri and Mahanandia, "Generation Z Entering the Workforce."

26 Mondres, "How Generation Z Is Changing Financial Services."

27 Ibid.

28 Marianne Gomez, Tiffany Mawhinney, and Kimberly Betts, "Understanding Gen Z in the Workplace," Deloitte, 2019, https://www2. deloitte.com/us/en/pages/consumer-business/articles/understanding-generation-z-in-the-workplace.html.

29 Merrick, "X, Y, Z."

30 Chillakuri and Mahanandia, "Generation Z Entering the Workforce."

31 Merrick, "X, Y, Z."

32 Deloitte, "Millennials and Generation Z – Making Mental Health at Work a Priority," *Deloitte Global Talent Report*, June 2021.

33 Chloe Berger, "Gen Zers Are Rebelling against Their Parents and Striking Fear into Corporate America by Publicly Quitting," *Fortune*, 19 March 2022.

34 Pilita Clark, "The Man Who Predicted the Great Resignation Has More Big News," *Financial Times*, 3 April 2022.

35 Berger, "Gen Zers Are Rebelling."

36 Jennifer Jordan and Michael Sorell, "Why Reverse Mentoring Works and How to Do It Right," *Harvard Business Review*, 3 October 2019.

37 Ryan Jenkin, "This Is How Generation Z Employees Want Feedback," *Inc.*, 25 June 2019.

38 Ibid.

39 Ibid.
40 Raisa Bruner, "Remote Work Is All That Gen Z Know. But Are They Satisfied?," *Time*, 16 August 2021.

CHAPTER ELEVEN

1 Liz Simpson, "Why Managing Up Matters," *Harvard Business Review*, 31 July 2002.
2 *Managing Up*, HBR 20-Minute Manager Series (Boston: Harvard Business Review Press, 2014).
3 This goes back to one of the classic articles in the field of managing upward: John Gabarro and John Kotter, "Managing Your Boss," *Harvard Business Review*, 1980. We don't use the word "boss" much anymore but it is an older article. One of the newer ideas is to think about our manager as an introvert, ambivert, or extrovert. Sound basic principles in this article but the world evolves.
4 Karl Moore, "'Never Apologize, Never Explain' and Other Bad Ideas for Working with Millennials," *The Globe and Mail*, 9 January 2018.
5 *Managing Up*.
6 Marshall makes the point that we should "focus on contributing to the greater good not just on achieving your objectives." Marshall Goldsmith, "How Can I Do a Better Job of Managing Upward," *Harvard Management Update*, 1 February 2008.
7 John J. Gabarro and John P. Kotter, "Managing Your Boss," *Harvard Business Review*, January 2005.
8 Amy Gallo, "Setting the Record Straight on Managing Your Boss," *Harvard Business Review*, 18 December 2014.

KEY POSTMODERN TERMS

1 Jean Baudrillard, *Simulations* (New York: Semiotext[e], 1983), 146.
2 Ibid., 2.
3 Jean Baudrillard, "Implosion of Meaning in the Media," in *In the Shadow of the Silent Majorities* (New York: Semiotext[e], 1983).

4 Baudrillard, *Simulations*, 57.

5 Zygmunt Bauman, "Philosophical Affinities of Postmodern Sociology," *Sociological Review* 38: 427.

6 Jacques Derrida, *Of Grammatology* (Baltimore and London: Johns Hopkins University Press, 1976), 49.

7 Ben Agger, *The Decline of Discourse: Reading, Writing, and Resistance in Postmodern Capitalism* (New York: Palmer Press, 1990), 214.

Further Reading

In writing this book, I researched a number of books, newspapers, and articles on Postmoderns (also known as Millennials, Generation Z, or the Net Generation). The following is a list of the most helpful.

BOOKS

Alsop, Ron. *The Trophy Kids Grow Up: How the Millennial Generation Is Shaking Up the Workplace.* San Francisco: Jossey-Bass, 2008. Providing a rich portrait of Millennials and how they represent a new breed of student, worker, and global citizen, this book describes how this remarkable generation promises to stir up the workplace and perhaps the world.

Ball, Ken, and Gina Gotsill. *Surviving the Baby Boomer Exodus: Capturing Knowledge for Gen X and Gen Y Employees.* Boston: Cengage Learning, 2011. Filled with scenarios, case studies, tips, templates, and checklists, this book presents methods for assessing a company's knowledge gaps, creating a knowledge transfer plan, and nurturing a culture that encourages knowledge sharing and collaboration.

Deal, Jennifer J., and Alec Robert Levenson. *What Millennials Want from Work: How to Maximize Engagement in Today's Workforce.* New York: McGraw Hill Education, 2016.

Dorsey, Jason R. *Y-Size Your Business: How Gen Y Employees Can Save You Money and Grow Your Business.* Hoboken, NJ: John Wiley & Sons, 2010. Authored by a member of Gen Y, this guide presents precisely the solutions you need to make the most of a generation growing in importance and ready to make an impact on your bottom line right away.

Erickson, Tamara J. *Plugged In: The Generation Y Guide to Thriving at Work.* Boston: Harvard Business Press, 2008. Filled with the author's extensive research into demographic trends and thoughtful insights, this book gives Gen Y the information they crave to connect with the working world and to craft the lives they want.

Espinoza, Chip, Mick Ukleja, and Craig Rusch. *Managing the Millennials: Discover the Core Competencies for Managing Today's Workforce.* Hoboken, NJ: John Wiley & Sons, 2010. Sharing relevant interviews, case studies, and offering research-backed ideas and best practices, this insightful and practical book answers the perplexing question: "How does one lead and manage younger employees?"

Fenn, Donna. *Upstarts! How GenY Entrepreneurs Are Rocking the World of Business and 8 Ways You Can Profit from Their Success.* New York: McGraw-Hill, 2010. Examining the Gen Y entrepreneurial revolution to reveal eight critical lessons every entrepreneur and marketer must learn, this book will help you adapt to the new way of business to give you a greater chance to grow and profit in the years ahead.

Fromm, Jeff, and Angie Read. *Marketing to Gen Z: The Rules for Reaching This Vast and Very Different Generation of Influencers.* New York: AMACOM, 2018.

Fromm, Jeff, and Christie Garton. *Marketing to Millennials: Reach the Largest and Most Influential Generation of Consumers Ever.* New York: AMACOM, 2013. Eighty million Millennials wielding $200 billion in buying power are entering their peak earning and spending years. The book reveals the eight attitudes shared by most Millennials, as well as the new rules for engaging them successfully.

Gallup, Inc. *How Millennials Want to Work and Live.* Washington, DC: Gallup, Inc., 2016.

Gravett, Linda S., and Robin Throckmorton. *Bridging the Generation Gap: How to Get Radio Babies, Boomers, Gen Xers, and Gen Yers to Work Together and Achieve More.* Franklin Lakes, NJ: Career Press, 2007. Filled with strategies and solutions you can implement immediately, this book offers real-life cases and ground-breaking research on how members of any generation can better relate to minimize conflict, miscommunication, and wasted energy.

Howe, Neil. *Millennials Rising: The Next Generation.* N.p.: Knopf Doubleday Group, 2009. Basic introduction of the Millennial generation including behaviours, personalities, and life perceptions. Excellent starting point for understanding Millennial mentality.

Hughes, Claretha. *Workforce Inter-Personnel Diversity: The Power to Influence Human Productivity and Career Development.* London: Palgrave Macmillan, 2019.

Johnson, Meagan, and Larry Johnson. *Generations, Inc.: From Boomers to Linksters – Managing the Friction between Generations at Work.* New York: AMACOM, 2010. Offering perspectives from people of different eras and eliciting practical insights on wrestling with generational issues in the workplace, this book provides realistic strategies for those seeking to coexist, flourish, and thrive together … at the same time.

Lancaster, Lynne C., and David Stillman. *The M-factor: How the Millennial Generation Is Rocking the Workplace.* New York: Harper Business, 2010. "What do these Millennials want? Why are they so different? How do we get the good ones in the door? How do we keep them there without alienating the other generations?" Going forward, a company's success will depend upon knowing the answers to these questions, because they are the keys to motivating this new generation and to taking advantage of the amazing potential it possesses.

Levit, Alexandra. *#Millennialtweet: 140 Bite-Sized Ideas for Managing the Millennials.* Cupertino, CA: Happy About, 2009. Quick and easy tips specifically oriented toward working more efficiently and effectively with Millennials.

Lipkin, Nicole A., and April J. Perrymore. *Y in the Workplace: Managing the "Me First" Generation.* Franklin Lakes, NJ: Career Press, 2009. With psychological insight into the character of this generation, this book illustrates how the values, attitudes, and expectations of Gen Y have had an impact on corporate environments, intergenerational functioning, and management strategies.

Marventano, Jessica, and Catherine Wallace. *The Marvelous Millennial's Manual to Modern Manners: Professional Success and Happiness with the Help of Business Etiquette.* New York: Morgan James Publishing, 2019.

Moos, Marcus, Deirdre Pfeiffer, and Tara Vinodrai. *The Millennial City: Trends, Implications, and Prospects for Urban Planning and Policy.* Abingdon, UK: Routledge, 2018.

Ng, Eddy S.W., Sean T. Lyons, and Linda Schweitzer. *Managing the New Workforce: International Perspectives on the Millennial Generation*. Cheltenham, UK: Edward Elgar Print, 2012. Millennials represent the workforce of the future and come with their own set of expectations, demands, and work habits. The contributors to this volume, drawn from countries around the world, document the cultural, historical, and social context surrounding this phenomenon.

Phillips, Kevin. *Managing Millennials: The Ultimate Handbook for Productivity, Profitability, and Professionalism*. New York: Taylor & Francis, 2018.

Pontefract, Dan. *The Purpose Effect*. Boise, ID: Elevate, 2016. Excellent book on purpose by Dan Pontefract, who is a senior executive at Telus, a giant Canadian telecom company.

Poswolsky, Adam S. *The Quarter-Life Breakthrough*. New York: Tarcher-Peerigee, 2016.

Quinn, Clark. *Millennials, Goldfish & Other Training Misconceptions: Debunking Learning Myths and Superstitions*. Alexandria, VA: ATD Press, 2018.

Seemiller, Corey, and Meghan Grace. *Generation Z : A Century in the Making*. Abingdon, UK: Routledge, 2019.

Sengupta, Debashish. *The Life of Y: Engaging Millennials as Employees and Consumers*. Thousand Oaks, CA: SAGE Publications, 2018.

Shandler, Donald. *Motivating the Millennial Knowledge Worker: Help Today's Workforce Succeed in Today's Economy*. Fairport, NY: Axzo, 2009. This book identifies the leadership skills necessary for not only cooperating with but also developing the fastest-growing future generation of workers.

Stark, David. *Reaching Millennials: Proven Methods for Engaging a Younger Generation*. Minneapolis: Bethany House, 2016.

Sujansky, Joanne, and Jan Ferri-Reed. *Keeping the Millennials: Why Companies Are Losing Billions in Turnover to This Generation – and What to Do about It*. Hoboken, NJ: John Wiley & Sons, 2009. If your company is struggling to hang on to young workers, this book offers sage advice and smart strategies for building a workplace that welcomes employees of every generation.

Tapscott, Don. *Grown Up Digital: How the Net Generation Is Changing Your World*. New York: McGraw-Hill, 2009. Inspired by a $4 million private research study of more than 11,000 young people, this book examines how today's Net Generation is changing every aspect of our society – from the workplace to the marketplace, from the voting booth to the Oval Office.

Taylor, Paul. *The Next America: Boomers, Millennials, and the Looming Generational Showdown*. New York: Public Affairs, 2016.

Tulgan, Bruce. *Not Everyone Gets a Trophy: How to Manage Generation Y*. San Francisco: Jossey-Bass, 2009. Debunking dozens of myths about Generation Y in the workforce, this unique book provides proven, step-by-step best practices for getting Gen Y on board and up to speed by teaching them how to manage themselves and how to be managed.

Tulgan, Bruce, and Carolyn A. Martin. *Managing Generation Y: Global Citizens Born in the Late Seventies and Early Eighties*. Amherst, MA: HRD Press, 2001. Discover the Gen Y traits that pose the greatest challenges to managers as well as the best practices you can implement now to keep these upbeat, tech-savvy workers focused and motivated.

JOURNAL ARTICLES

Alsop, Ron. "Talking B-school: Welcoming the New Millennials; M.B.A. Programs Adjust to the Next Generation, and Their Parents." *Wall Street Journal* (2007): B.9–B.9. https://search.proquest.com/docview/3990 47434?accountid=12339.

Abii, Francesca E., David C.N. Ogula, and Jonathan M. Rose. "Effects of Individual and Organizational Factors on the Turnover Intentions of Information Technology Professionals." *International Journal of Management* 30, no. 2 (2013): 740–56.

Allen, David G. "Retaining Talent: A Guide to Analyzing and Managing Employee Turnover." *SHRM Foundation* (2008): 1–43. www.shrm.org/hr-today/trends-and-forecasting/special-reports-and-expert-views/Documents/Retaining-Talent.pdf.

Baroudi, Jack J. "The Impact of Role Variables on IS Personnel Work Attitudes and Intentions." *MIS Quarterly* 9 (1985): 341–55.

Basford, Tessa, and Bill Schaninger. "Winning Hearts and Minds in the 21st Century." *McKinsey Quarterly* (2016): 122–6.

Brum, Scott. "What Impact Does Training Have on Employee Commitment and Employee Turnover?" *Schmidt Labor Research Center Seminar Paper Series, University of Rhode Island* (2007).

Erickson, Tamara J. "The Leaders We Need Now." *Harvard Business Review* 88, no. 5 (2010): 62–6.

Erickson, Tamara J., R. Alsop, Pamela Nicholson, and J. Miller. "Gen Y in the Workforce." *Harvard Business Review* 87, no. 2 (2009): 43–9. Retrieved from EBSCOhost.

Farooq, Miriam. "Organizational Justice, Employee Turnover, and Trust in the Workplace: A Study in South Asian Telecommunication Companies." *Global Business and Organizational Excellence* 33, no. 3 (2014).

Goldstein, David K., and John F. Rockart. "An Examination of Work-Related Correlates of Job Satisfaction in Programmer and Analysts." *MIS Quarterly* 8 (1984): 103–15.

Joshi, Aparna, John C. Dencker, Gentz Franz, and Joseph J. Martocchio. "Unpacking Generational Identities in Organizations." *Academy of Management Review* 35, no. 3 (2010): 392–414.

Kamal, Mustafa. "Information Technology Workforce – Planning for the Future." *Journal of American Academy of Business* 7, no. 2 (2005): 23–6.

Kazi, Ghulam Mustafa, and Zainab F. Zadeh. "The Contribution of Individual Variables: Job Satisfaction and Job Turnover." *Interdisciplinary Journal of Contemporary Research in Business* 3, no. 5 (2011): 984–91.

Ladelsky, Limor Kessler, and Gheorghe Alexandru Catana. "Causes Affecting Voluntary Turnover in IT Sector." *International Conference "Marketing – from Information to Decision,"* 6th edition (2013): 102–13.

Li-Ping Tang, Thomas, Jwa K. Kim, and David Shin-Hsiung Tang. "Does Attitude toward Money Moderate the Relationship between Intrinsic Job Satisfaction and Voluntary Turnover?" *SAGE Publications* 53, no. 2 (2000): 213–45.

Maas, Judith. "Generations at Work: Managing the Clash of Veterans, Boomers, Xers, and Nexters in Your Workplace." *Sloan Management Review* 41, no. 2 (2000): 98–9.

Meister, Jeanne C., and Karie Willyerd. "Mentoring Millennials." *Harvard Business Review* 88, no. 5 (2010): 68–72.

Tariq, Muhammad Naeem, Muhammad Ramzan, and Aisha Riaz. "The Impact of Employee Turnover on the Efficiency of the Organization."

Interdisciplinary Journal of Contemporary Research in Business 4, no. 9 (2013): 700–11.

Pare, Guy, Michel Tremblay, and Patrick Lalonde. "The Role of Organizational Commitment and Citizenship Behaviours in Understanding Relations between Human Resources Practices and Turnover Intentions of IT Personnel." *Cirano*, 2001.

Pfau, Bruce N. "What Do Millennials Really Want at Work? The Same Things the Rest of Us Do." *Harvard Business Review*, 2016.

Shropshire, Jordan, and Christopher Kaldec. "I'm Leaving the IT Field: The Impact of Stress, Job Insecurity, and Burnout on IT Professionals." *International Journal of Information and Communication Technology Research* 2, no. 1 (2012): 6–16.

Su, Amy Jen, and Muriel Maignan Wilkins. "What Gets in the Way of Listening." *Harvard Business Review*, 14 April 2014.

Twenge, Jean M., Stacy M. Campbell, Brian J. Hoffman, and Charles E. Lance. "Generational Differences in Work Values: Leisure and Extrinsic Values Increasing, Social and Intrinsic Values Decreasing." *Journal of Management* 36, no. 5 (2010): 1117–42.

Zaczkiewicz, Arthur. "Listen Up: What It Takes to Manage Millennials." *WWD*, 2016.

NEWSPAPERS

Ante, Spencer E. "Offering Advice Free of Charge." *Wall Street Journal*, 6 December 2010. https://www.wsj.com/articles/SB10001424052748703350104575653244220509622.

Berkow, Jameson. "Canadian IT Sector Facing 'Alarming' Labour Shortage: Report." *Financial Post*, 29 March 2011. https://financialpost.com/technology/canadian-it-sector-to-face-alarming-labour-shortages-study.

Carey, Benedict. "A Snapshot of a Generation May Come Out Blurry." *The New York Times*, 3 August 2010. https://www.nytimes.com/2010/08/03/health/03mind.html.

Casey, Michael Jr. "Generation 'Y Me?'" *The Wall Street Journal*, 22 January 2011. https://www.wsj.com/articles/SB100014240527487039893045755042629970833390.

Chokshi, Niraj. "How Badly Companies Misunderstand Millennials."
    Washington Post, 11 May 2016. https://www.washingtonpost.com/news/
    wonk/wp/2016/05/11/how-badly-companies-misunderstand-millennials/.
Cody, Steve. "5 Tricks for Working with Millennials." *Inc.*, 18 April 2013.
    https://www.inc.com/steve-cody/dealing-with-millennial-employees.html.
Cohen, Norma. "Young Generations Face Wealth Deficit." *Financial Times*,
    17 February 2010. https://www.ft.com/content/c3cc07bc-1b3c-11df-953f-
    00144feab49a.
Donkin, Richard. "Caught Somewhere between the Ys and the Boomers."
    Financial Times, 31 December 2009. Retrieved from www.ft.com/home/uk.
Echler, Leah. "For Younger Workers, Perks Trump Pay." *The Globe and Mail*,
    13 September 2013. https://www.theglobeandmail.com/report-on-busi
    ness/careers/career-advice/life-at-work/for-younger-workers-perks-
    trump-pay/article14317896/.
Eng, Dinah. "What Do Millennials Want? Hotels Have Some Ideas." *The
    New York Times*, 4 April 2016. https://www.nytimes.com/2016/04/10/
    travel/millennials-hotels.html.
Fandos, Nicholas. "Connections to a Cause: The Millennial Way of
    Charity." *The New York Times*, 3 November 2016. https://www.nytimes.
    com/2016/11/06/giving/connections-to-a-cause-the-millennial-way-of-
    charity.html.
Friese, Lauren. "Millennials: Why 'Celebrate Everything' Is Good Career
    Advice." *The Globe and Mail*, 8 November 2016. https://www.theglobeand
    mail.com/globe-investor/personal-finance/genymoney/millennials-why-
    you-should-strive-to-fail-at-work/article32700303/.
Gatti, Kat. "Let's Rebrand the Millennial Generation, from Lazy and Enti-
    tled to One that Never Gives Up." *The Globe and Mail*, 8 January 2015.
    https://www.theglobeandmail.com/life/facts-and-arguments/rebranding-
    the-millennial-generation-we-should-never-give-up/article22336873/.
Gilbert, Mandy. "Five Strategies to Help Keep the Job-Hopping Generation
    Working for You." *Financial Post*, 15 September 2016. https://financial
    post.com/executive/careers/five-strategies-to-help-keep-the-job-hopping-
    generation-working-for-you.
– "How to Invest in Your Employees beyond Giving a Raise." *Financial Post*,
    26 May 2016. https://financialpost.com/entrepreneur/small-business/
    how-to-invest-in-your-employees-beyond-giving-a-raise.

Goldsmith, Marshall. "Five Global Leadership Factors." *Bloomberg*, 13 October 2009. https://www.bloomberg.com/news/articles/2009-10-13/five-global-leadership-factors.

Gould, John. "The Economic Indicators That Shaped Three Generations." *Wall Street Journal*, Dow Jones & Company, 12 March 2020. https://www.wsj.com/articles/the-economic-indicators-that-shaped-three-generations-11583975591.

Gourani, Soulaima. "Leading Multiple Generations in Today's Workforce." *Forbes*, 25 April 2019. https://www.forbes.com/sites/soulaimagourani/2019/04/25/leading-multiple-generations-in-todays-workforce/?sh=7a5e89ce4636.

Hayzlett, Jeffrey. "4 Ways Employers Are Using Corporate Social Responsibility to Recruit Millennials." *Entrepreneur*, 25 November 2016. https://www.entrepreneur.com/leadership/4-ways-employers-are-using-corporate-social-responsibility/285587.

Hite, Brittany. "Employers Rethink How They Give Feedback." *The Wall Street Journal*. 13 October 2008. Retrieved from www.wsj.com.

Hoover, Margaret. "How the GOP Can Win Young Voters." *The Wall Street Journal*, 22 July 2011. https://www.wsj.com/articles/SB10001424052702303661904576455723288613268.

Hughes, Jazmine. "Need to Keep Gen Z Workers Happy? Hire a 'Generational Consultant.'" *The New York Times*, 20 February 2020. https://www.nytimes.com/interactive/2020/02/19/magazine/millennials-gen-z-consulting.html.

Indap, Sujeet. "Estée Lauder Applies Millennial Makeover." *Financial Times*, 17 November 2016. https://www.ft.com/content/e98d3ada-9acd-11e6-8f9b-70e3cabccfae.

Jacobs, Emma. "Three Generations in One Office." *Financial Times*, 23 October 2014. https://www.ft.com/content/ab8ad1a4-5847-11e4-a31b-00144feab7de.

Johnson, Gail. "Millennials Need Purpose, Not Ping-Pong." *The Globe and Mail*, 23 March 2016. https://www.theglobeandmail.com/report-on-business/millennials-need-purpose-not-ping-pong/article29337726/.

King, Eden, et al. "Just How Different Are Millennials, Gen Xers, and Baby Boomers at Work?" *Harvard Business Review*, 2 August 2019. https://hbr.org/2019/08/generational-differences-at-work-are-small-thinking-theyre-big-affects-our-behavior.

Kreamer, Anne. "Taking Your Feelings to Work." *The New York Times*, 12 June 2011. https://www.nytimes.com/2011/06/12/jobs/12pre.html.

Krook, Dana. "One in Three Employees Don't Trust Their Employer – How to Change That at Your Company." *Financial Post*, 12 August 2016. Retrieved from www.business.financialpost.com.

Leahy, Joe. "Recognizing a Marketable Trend." *Financial Times*, 2 September 2010. Retrieved from www.ft.com/home/uk.

Maddeaux, Sabrina. "Rise of the Millennial Philanthropists: This Generation Is Eager to Give Back Despite Its Reputation." *National Post*, 18 October 2016. Retrieved from http://news.nationalpost.com.

Manjoo, Farhad. "Corporate America Chases the Mythical Millennial." *The New York Times*, 25 May 2016. https://www.nytimes.com/2016/05/26/technology/corporate-america-chases-the-mythical-millennial.html.

Martínez-Cabrera, Alejandro. "'Millennials' Leading the Way on Social Media." sfgate, 9 July 2010. https://www.sfgate.com/business/article/Millennials-leading-the-way-on-social-media-3182542.php.

Meister, Jeanne. "Job Hopping Is the 'New Normal' for Millennials: Three Ways to Prevent a Human Resource Nightmare." *Forbes*, 14 August 2012. https://www.forbes.com/sites/jeannemeister/2012/08/14/the-future-of-work-job-hopping-is-the-new-normal-for-millennials/.

Miller, Claire Cain, and Sanam Yar. "Young People Are Going to Save Us All from Office Life." *The New York Times*, 17 September 2019. https://www.nytimes.com/2019/09/17/style/generation-z-millennials-work-life-balance.html.

Mims, Christopher. "Generation Z's 7 Lessons for Surviving in Our Tech-Obsessed World." *The Wall Street Journal*, 26 January 2019. https://www.wsj.com/articles/generation-zs-7-lessons-for-surviving-in-our-tech-obsessed-world-11548478811.

Muther, Christopher. "The Growing Culture of Impatience Makes Us Crave More and More Instant Gratification." *The Boston Globe*, 2 February 2013. https://www.bostonglobe.com/lifestyle/style/2013/02/01/the-growing-culture-impatience-where-instant-gratification-makes-crave-more-instant-gratification/q8tWDNGeJB2mm45fQxtTQP/story.html.

Olson, Elizabeth. "For Millennials, It's More about Personal Style than Luxury." *The New York Times*, 2 November 2010. https://www.nytimes.com/2010/11/03/business/media/03adco.html.

Pearson, Mia. "Young Entrepreneurs and the Myth of the Lazy Millennial." *The Globe and Mail*, 26 September 2016. https://www.theglobeandmail. com/report-on-business/small-business/sb-marketing/young-entre preneurs-and-the-myth-of-the-lazy-millennial/article31989890/.

Popper, Nathaniel. "Young Adults, Burdened with Debt, Are Now Facing an Economic Crisis." *The New York Times*, 6 April 2020. https://www.ny times.com/2020/04/06/business/millennials-economic-crisis-virus.html.

Rampell, Catherine. "A Generation of Slackers? Not So Much." *The New York Times*, 29 May 2011. https://www.nytimes.com/2011/05/29/weekin review/29graduates.html.

Sardon, Maitane. "A Guarded Generation: How Millennials View Money and Investing." *The Wall Street Journal*, 13 March 2020. https://www.wsj. com/articles/the-recession-left-millennials-loaded-with-debtand-cynical-11583956727.

Siegel, Rachel, and Andrew Van Dam. "How Gen X, Millennials and Gen Z Became the Low- Inflation Generations." *The Washington Post*, 10 December 2019. https://www.washingtonpost.com/business/2019/12/10/how-gen-x-millennials-gen-z-became-low-inflation-generations/.

Suarez, J. Gerald. "A Baby Boomer's Guide to Managing Millennials at Work." *Los Angeles Times*, 24 November 2016. https://www.latimes.com/business/la-fi-career-coach-boomers-millennials-20161124-story.html.

– "Career Coach: Boomers, Know Thy Millennial." *The Washington Post*, 11 November 2016. Retrieved from www.washingtonpost.com.

Teitel, Emma. "Proof that Millennials Work Just as Hard as Boomers: Teitel." *Toronto Star*, 27 November 2016. www.thestar.com/news/canada/2016/11/02/proof-that-Millennials-work-just-as-hard-as-boomers-teitel.html.

Uchitelle, Louis. "A New Generation, an Elusive American Dream." *The New York Times*, 7 July 2010. https://www.nytimes.com/2010/07/07/busi ness/economy/07generation.html.

Warner, Judith. "The Why-Worry Generation." *The New York Times*, 30 May 2010. https://www.nytimes.com/2010/05/30/magazine/30fob-wwln-t.html.

Widdicombe, Ben. "What Happens When Millennials Run the Workplace?" *The New York Times*, 19 March 2016. https://www.nytimes.com/2016/03/20/fashion/millennials-mic-workplace.html.

Zaczkiewicz, Arthur. "Listen Up: What It Takes to Manage Millennials."

WWD, 5 April 2016. https://wwd.com/business-news/human-resources/
millennials-workplace-retail-executives-10403822/.

Zimmer, Ben. "'OK Boomer': A Defining Generation Becomes a Label for
Irrelevance." *The Wall Street Journal*, 21 December 2019. https://www.wsj.
com/articles/ok-boomer-a-defining-generation-becomes-a-label-for-ir
relevance-11576904461.

– "'Z' Is for the Post-Millennial Generation." *The Wall Street Journal*,
1 February 2019. https://www.wsj.com/articles/z-is-for-the-post-
millennial-generation-11549045923.

Index

post-truth, 37–9

purpose: communicating, 87; organizational, 86–7; personal, 87; sense of, 77, 86

Quiet Leadership Institute, 9

retention: among Millennial/Gen Z, 70; patient, 31; in public service, 47

reverse mentoring, 102; alternative strategies for, 107–9; definition of, 102; key benefits of, 103–5, 109

self: lost, 70; regained, 72

shareholders to stakeholders, shift from, 87, 144

social media: as research tool, 117; as surrogate parent, 118

strategy: deliberate, 131; emergent, 131–3, 147; and leadership, 42; optimal, 58; viable, 57. *See also* Dempsey, General Martin; Mintzberg, Henry; Porter, Michael

technology, influence on knowledge acquisition, 15

truth, 10, 29; changing nature of, 36–8; interpreting, 39–40; universal, 36

Truth: universal, 38

value chains: problems with, 5; shared, 132

voices: privileging all, 50

war: for talent, 12

War: Second World, 5; Vietnam, 7, 36

wisdom, liquid and crystallized, 15–16

workforce, several generations in the, 14

work-life: balance, 69; integration, 17, 82, 91, 112

workplace: changes in, 34; changing values, 34; emotions, 43; fundamental shift in, 12; hierarchical approach in, 22; managing Postmoderns in, 33. *See also* workforce

worldview, 4, 5, 6, 7, 10; Modern, 18, 19; Postmodern, 22